Canon EOS 90D User Guide for Beginners and Seniors

Master Camera Buttons, Autofocus Modes, and 4K Video Settings with Step-by-Step Instructions, Photography Tricks, and Real-Life Shooting Tips

Randy Osborn

Copyright © 2025 by Randy Osborn

Disclaimer:

This book is an independent publication and is not affiliated with, authorized by, sponsored by, or endorsed by Canon Inc. or any of its subsidiaries. Canon®, EOS®, and any related model names, logos, and branding are trademarks or registered trademarks of Canon Inc., which are used solely for descriptive and educational purposes.

All product names, logos, and brands mentioned in this book are the property of their respective owners. The information contained in this guide is based on publicly available resources, personal experience, research, and practical testing. It is intended for educational and informational purposes only and should not be considered official Canon documentation.

While every effort has been made to ensure the accuracy and usefulness of the content, the author and publisher make no warranties or representations regarding the completeness, reliability, or applicability of the techniques, settings, or recommendations presented. The use of any camera gear or shooting method is solely at the reader's discretion and risk.

Always consult the official Canon user manual or authorized Canon support for up-to-date product specifications, firmware changes, and warranty-related concerns.

By reading this book, you acknowledge that the author and publisher shall not be held liable for any loss, damage, or injury resulting from the use or misuse of the information provided.

Table of Contents

Preface

Unlock the full potential of your DSLR with the most complete Canon EOS 90D User Guide available.

Whether you're searching for a *Canon 90D Manual*, a step-by-step setup tutorial, or insider tips for breathtaking photography and video, this book is designed for beginners, seniors, travelers, and creators who want results without the overwhelm.

This Canon EOS 90D for Beginners and Canon EOS 90D for Seniors handbook goes far beyond the official manual. Inside, you'll find a Canon EOS 90D Photography Guide and Canon EOS 90D Video Guide rolled into one—covering everything from Canon 90D Camera Settings and focusing techniques to creative shooting projects and post-shoot workflows. This isn't just another generic Canon 90D DSLR Camera Book; it's your friendly coach, walking you through how to use Canon EOS 90D in real-life situations.

Learn the secrets behind perfect Canon EOS 90D Autofocus Settings, follow our Canon EOS 90D 4K Video Tutorial to create cinematic YouTube content, and discover the best lenses for Canon EOS 90D whether you're shooting portraits, landscapes, wildlife, or action sports. Packed with Canon 90D tips and tricks, this guide includes a Canon EOS 90D Setup Step-by-Step process, insider advice for Canon EOS 90D Low Light Photography, Canon EOS 90D Wildlife Photography, and Canon EOS 90D Portrait Settings that make your images pop straight out of the camera.

With easy photography tutorials for Canon EOS 90D, even total beginners will feel confident. Whether you need a Canon EOS 90D Beginners Photography Book for stills, or the best Canon 90D guide for YouTube videos and vlogging, you'll learn how to shoot video with Canon EOS 90D that's smooth, sharp, and ready to share. There's also a complete Canon EOS 90D Manual for Travel Photography, perfect for on-the-go creators who want lightweight, high-quality shooting setups.

From Canon EOS 90D for Action and Sports Shots to stunning sunsets, we include step-by-step Canon EOS 90D photography lessons and a practical Canon EOS 90D Tips for Seniors and New Users section so everyone can enjoy their camera without the learning curve.

Inside, you'll also find:

- A complete canon eos 90d user guide manual beginners seniors photography approach that's jargon-free.

- A canon 90d camera book step by step autofocus video setup tips section for quick mastery.

- Guides on how to use canon eos 90d dslr wildlife portrait low light shots for every scenario.

- A canon eos 90d photography tutorial travel youtube vlogging guide for hybrid shooters.

- A canon 90d manual for beginners seniors best lens settings tricks chapter for upgrading your kit affordably.

- Easy photography tutorials canon eos 90d 4k video slow motion shooting techniques explained clearly.

- A canon eos 90d setup step-by-step buttons dials menu functions reference so you never miss a setting.

Whether you're picking up the Canon EOS 90D for the first time or looking to push its limits, this book will turn your camera into a tool you can truly master. Say goodbye to missed shots and confusing menus—say hello to confident shooting in any condition.

If you want the ultimate photography and video companion for your Canon EOS 90D—this is it.

Introduction

Why This Camera and This Book Will Change the Way You Shoot

If you've just unboxed your Canon EOS 90D—or maybe you've had it for a while but haven't ventured far beyond the Auto setting—welcome. You've joined a community of photographers and creators who chose this camera for a reason: it's powerful, versatile, and capable of capturing moments in extraordinary detail. But if you're feeling a little overwhelmed by its many buttons, menus, and features, you're not alone.

Whether you're a beginner taking your first steps in photography, a senior rediscovering the joy of capturing life's moments, or someone upgrading from a simpler camera, the EOS 90D can feel like a lot to take in. The good news is, you don't have to be technical to take stunning photos and videos. You don't need to memorize every page of the official Canon manual or understand every piece of photography jargon to get the results you want. All you need is a clear, simple, and practical path forward—one that shows you exactly what to do and why it works. That's where this book comes in.

The official Canon EOS 90D manual is an impressive technical document, but it's designed to cover every possible function in every possible situation, often in language that can feel more like an engineering report than a friendly guide. If you've ever flipped through it only to set it aside in frustration, you're not alone. Many 90D owners want something different: a guide that speaks to real people, uses plain English, and focuses on how to use the camera in real-world situations—from photographing a family birthday to recording a travel vlog, from capturing your grandkids in motion to photographing a sunset without losing the colors you see with your own eyes.

This book has been written to be that guide. You'll find no unnecessary jargon, no intimidating walls of text, and no assumption that you've been shooting for decades. Instead, you'll discover:

- Step-by-step instructions for setting up and using your 90D without overwhelm.

- Clear explanations of important camera functions, translated into everyday terms.

- Ready-to-use shooting setups for common situations so you can get great results immediately.

- Practical tips for autofocus, video recording, and creative photography that you can actually apply.

- Troubleshooting solutions for the most common frustrations owners face.

Think of this as a conversation with a patient photography coach who's sitting right beside you, walking you through exactly what to do. Each chapter is designed to solve a problem you might encounter with your 90D, helping you go from "I hope I get the shot" to "I know I've got it" in the shortest time possible.

By the time you've finished, your Canon EOS 90D will no longer feel like a complicated piece of technology—it will feel like a natural extension of your eye and imagination. You'll know how to make it work for *your* needs, in *your* style, and at *your* pace. And you might just find that the joy of photography isn't in knowing every technical detail, but in having the confidence to capture life exactly the way you see it.

So let's begin. Your journey to confident, creative photography starts here.

Part 1: Getting Started Without Overwhelm

Chapter 1

Meet Your Canon EOS 90D – A Friendly Tour

If you've ever opened a new camera box and felt like you were staring at a spaceship's control panel, take a deep breath—you're in the right place. This chapter is all about getting you comfortable with the Canon EOS 90D. We'll take a no-pressure walk around the camera, explore what each button and dial does in plain English, learn how to hold it for rock-steady shots, and walk through a simple first-time setup so you're ready to start shooting confidently.

Getting to Know Your EOS 90D

The Canon EOS 90D is a DSLR camera—that means it has a mirror system inside, an optical viewfinder you look through, and the ability to change lenses. It's built for both photography and video, with powerful autofocus, a high-resolution 32.5-megapixel sensor, and the ability to shoot 4K video without cropping your frame.

Think of it as a multi-tool for creativity—whether you're photographing your family, wildlife, or your latest trip, it has the flexibility to handle it all. The good news is, you don't need to learn everything at once. Just like learning to drive, you can start with the basics and add more skills over time.

A Simple Walk Around Your Camera

Instead of throwing technical names at you, let's break down the main parts and what they *actually* do in everyday language.

Top of the Camera

1. **Mode Dial** – This is like the gear selector in a car. You choose whether you're driving automatic (Auto, Scene modes) or manual (M, Av, Tv). We'll talk more about modes in later chapters.

2. **Main Dial** – Near the shutter button, this dial changes settings like shutter speed or aperture, depending on the mode you're in.

3. **Shutter Button** – The big silver button you press to take a photo. Half-press to focus, press fully to shoot.

4. **On/Off Switch** – Simple, but easy to overlook. Flip it to start your creative journey.

5. **LCD Panel** – Displays quick information about your settings without having to look at the main screen.

Front of the Camera

1. **Lens Mount** – Where your lens connects to the camera body. Press the small release button beside it to swap lenses.

2. **Lens Release Button** – Lets you detach a lens safely.

3. **Self-Timer/Remote Sensor** – Detects signals from a remote or blinks when you're using a timer.

Back of the Camera

1. **Viewfinder** – The little window you look through to frame your shot in real time.

2. **LCD Touchscreen** – Fully articulating and touch-sensitive. Great for vlogging, selfies, or shooting at tricky angles.

3. **Menu Button** – Opens the camera's settings menu.

4. **Q (Quick) Button** – Gives you faster access to frequently used settings.

5. **Playback Button** – Lets you review photos and videos.

6. **AF-ON Button** – For activating autofocus without touching the shutter button—handy for action shots.

7. **Joystick/Multicontroller** – Lets you move the focus point around the frame.

Sides of the Camera

1. **Memory Card Slot** – On the right-hand grip side. The 90D uses SD cards—more on the best ones in Chapter 9.

2. **Ports** – On the left side under rubber flaps. Includes microphone input, headphone jack, HDMI output, USB, and remote control input.

How to Hold Your Camera for Steady Shots

One of the fastest ways to improve photo sharpness—without touching a single setting—is learning to hold your camera correctly.

1. **Grip with your right hand**: Wrap your fingers around the front grip, with your index finger on the shutter button.
2. **Support with your left hand**: Place it under the lens, not the side, to help with balance.
3. **Tuck your elbows in**: Rest them lightly against your body for stability.
4. **Stand with one foot slightly forward**: This helps you stay steady.
5. **Exhale gently as you shoot**: Just like a marksman—it reduces shake.

If you're shooting video or using a heavy lens, consider a neck strap or wrist strap for extra safety.

First-Time Setup Checklist

Before you take your first shot, let's make sure your 90D is set up for success.

1. **Charge the Battery** – Use the included charger and give it a full charge before first use.

2. **Insert the Memory Card** – Push it in until it clicks. Make sure it's an SD card with a good write speed for video.

3. **Turn the Camera On** – Flip the power switch to "On."

4. **Set the Date, Time, and Language** – The camera will prompt you the first time you power up. This keeps your photos organized by date and ensures the menus are easy to follow.

5. **Format the Memory Card** – In the menu, go to *Setup* → *Format Card*. This clears the card and prepares it for the camera.

6. **Set Image Quality** – Start with JPEG Fine for simplicity, or RAW+JPEG if you plan to learn editing later.

7. **Activate Touchscreen Controls** – Makes menu navigation quicker, especially for beginners.

8. **Enable Grid Display** – Found in *Display Settings*, this helps with composition straight away.

9. **Set Auto Power Off** – Saves battery when the camera is idle.

10. **Take a Test Shot** – Point at something nearby, half-press the shutter to focus, and press fully to capture.

Your First Connection With the 90D

Now that your Canon EOS 90D is powered up, set, and ready to go, you're already ahead of most new owners. The key takeaway from this first chapter is simple: the 90D isn't a mysterious, complicated machine—it's a tool built for you. The more you treat it like a familiar companion rather than a technical puzzle, the faster your

confidence will grow.

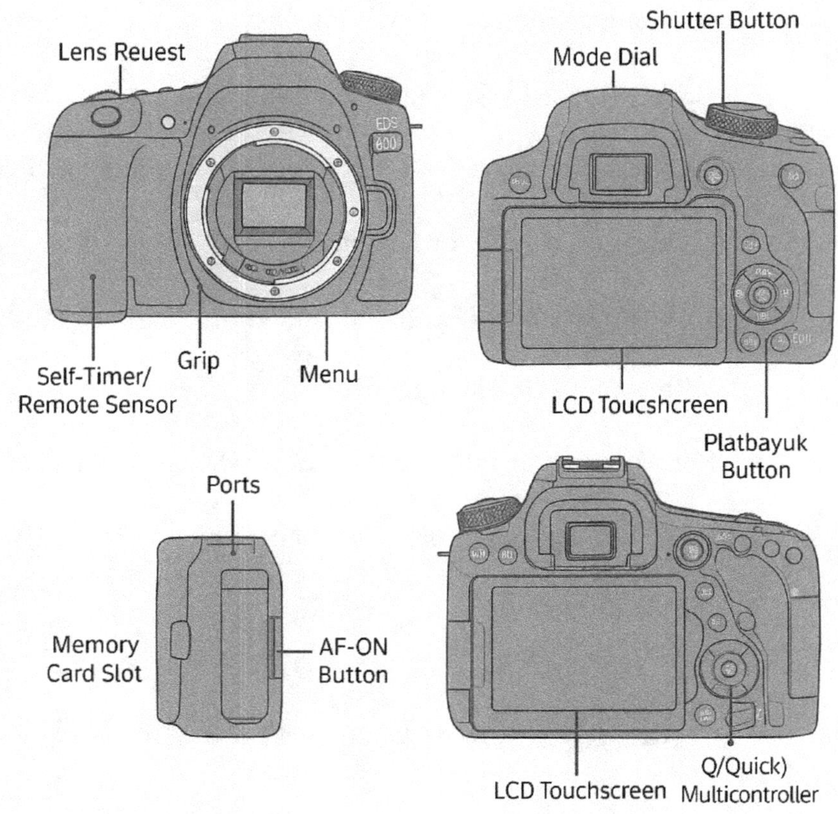

Chapter 2

Quick Start: Your Everyday Shooting Setup

One of the biggest frustrations for new Canon EOS 90D owners is feeling like they need to adjust a dozen settings every time they want to take a picture. The truth is, you don't have to. In this chapter, we'll create a go-to everyday shooting setup — a set of ready-to-use defaults that will give you beautiful results in 90% of situations without fiddling through menus. We'll also learn how to save these settings to a custom mode, so you can call them up instantly. Finally, we'll create three quick presets for the most common situations: indoor family shots, outdoor travel photography, and quick vlogging.

Your Everyday Shooting Setup

Think of this as your "baseline" camera setup — the starting point for most of your photography. You can tweak it for special situations, but these settings will give you a reliable, high-quality shot in most lighting and subjects.

Set these now:

1. **Mode** → *Av (Aperture Priority)*

   o Why: Lets you control background blur while the camera adjusts shutter speed automatically.

   o Good for: Everyday life, portraits, landscapes.

2. **Aperture** → *f/5.6*

   o Why: A sweet spot for sharpness and a pleasing depth of field.

3. **ISO** → *Auto (Max 3200)*

   o Why: Keeps your images bright without too much noise in most conditions.

4. **White Balance** → *Auto*

   o Why: Works well in varied lighting; can fine-tune later if needed.

5. **Focus Mode** → *One-Shot AF*

   o Why: Ideal for stationary subjects; gives a confirmation beep when focused.

6. **AF Area Mode** → *Face + Tracking*

   o Why: Keeps focus locked on faces, great for people and pets.

7. **Image Quality** → *JPEG Fine* (or RAW+JPEG if you plan to edit later).

8. **Metering Mode** → *Evaluative*

   o Why: Measures light across the whole frame for balanced exposure.

9. **Drive Mode** → *Single Shot*

   o Why: Prevents accidental bursts.

10. **Stabilization** → On (via lens switch)

   o Why: Helps keep shots sharp in handheld shooting.

Saving to a Custom Mode

The EOS 90D has three Custom Shooting Modes on the Mode Dial: *C1*, *C2*, and *C3*. You can store all your current settings in one of these so they're ready at a twist of the dial.

To save your Everyday Shooting Setup:

1. Set your camera to all the settings above.

2. Press Menu.

3. Go to Setup Tab (yellow wrench) → *Custom shooting mode (C1-C3)*.

4. Select Register settings.

5. Choose *C1* and press Set.

Now, whenever you turn the Mode Dial to *C1*, the camera instantly recalls your everyday settings.

Quick Presets for Common Scenarios

1. Indoor Family Shots

- **Mode:** Av

- **Aperture:** f/2.8 (lets in more light, nice background blur).

- **ISO:** Auto (Max 6400) — higher ISO to handle dim rooms.

- **White Balance:** Auto or Tungsten (if under warm indoor lighting).

- **Focus Mode:** One-Shot AF with Face + Tracking.

- **Tip:** If kids or pets are moving fast, switch to AI Servo for continuous focus.

- **Save to:** *C2* on the Mode Dial.

2. Outdoor Travel Shots

- **Mode:** Av

- **Aperture:** f/8 (sharp for landscapes and cityscapes).

- **ISO:** Auto (Max 800).

- **White Balance:** Daylight.

- **Focus Mode:** One-Shot AF.

- **AF Area:** Large Zone AF (to capture wide scenes).

- **Tip:** Use grid lines to keep horizons straight.

- **Save to:** *C3* on the Mode Dial.

3. Quick Vlogging Setup

- **Mode:** Movie Mode (flip the switch near the viewfinder).

- **Resolution:** 4K, 30fps (good balance of quality and smooth motion).

- **AF Mode:** Face + Tracking with Eye Detection.

- **Sound:** External mic plugged in (if available).

- **Stabilization:** Enable Digital IS (in Movie Settings).

- **Tip:** Flip the screen forward so you can see yourself while recording.

Why This Works

By creating a dependable Everyday Shooting Setup and assigning specific custom modes for your most common scenarios, you:

- Spend less time in menus.

- Avoid missing moments while fiddling with settings.

- Reduce the learning curve and build confidence.

- Keep your camera ready for any situation you face.

QUICK START: YOUR EVERYDAY SHOOTING SETUP

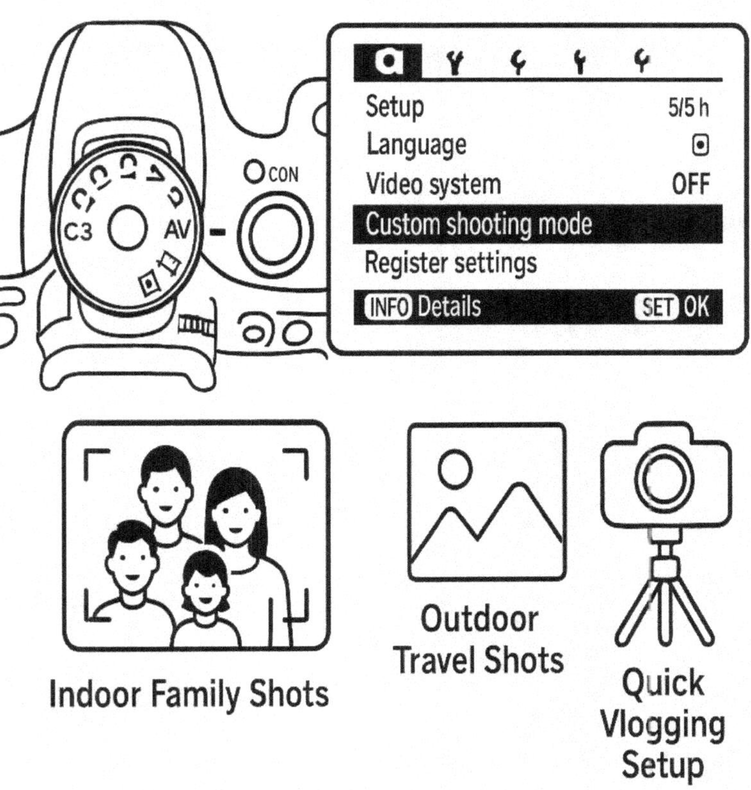

Part 2: Solving Common Shooting Problems

Chapter 3

Tackling Blurry Photos — Focus Made Simple

Few things are more disappointing than reviewing your shots and finding that the moment you wanted to capture—the smile, the goal, the jump—turned out soft, fuzzy, or completely out of focus. The Canon EOS 90D has one of the best autofocus systems in its class, but like any tool, it can only perform as well as the settings you give it. In this chapter, we'll break down why photos turn out blurry, how to choose the right autofocus mode for the situation, and how to make your 90D's focus tracking work for you instead of against you.

Why Photos Turn Out Blurry

Before we dive into settings, it's important to know the two main reasons images lack sharpness:

1. **Focus Missed the Subject**

   o The autofocus locked onto the wrong point (e.g., the background instead of your child's face).

   o Common when the subject is moving or when the AF mode isn't suited for the scene.

2. **Camera Shake or Subject Movement**

   o Even if the focus is correct, a slow shutter speed can cause motion blur.

   o This is especially common in low-light conditions when the camera slows down the shutter to let in more light.

Quick Fix Mindset:

- If the blur is from *focus issues*, change your autofocus mode or point selection.

- If the blur is from *movement*, adjust your shutter speed or use stabilization.

When to Use One-Shot AF, AI Servo, and Eye Detection

The 90D offers several autofocus modes, but these three will cover almost every real-world scenario.

1. One-Shot AF (Still Subjects)

- **When to Use:** Portraits, landscapes, still objects, posed group shots.

- **How It Works:** Locks focus when you half-press the shutter; the focus stays fixed until you take the shot.

- **Best For:** Stationary subjects where you have time to compose.

Pro Tip: Pair One-Shot AF with Face + Tracking AF method for portraits. It will lock onto faces automatically.

2. AI Servo AF (Moving Subjects)

- **When to Use:** Kids playing, pets running, sports, wildlife.

- **How It Works:** Continuously adjusts focus as the subject moves.

- **Best For:** Any subject that won't stay still, especially when moving toward or away from you.

Pro Tip: Combine AI Servo with Zone AF to keep focus on the moving target without constantly re-aiming your camera.

3. Eye Detection AF (People & Pets)

- **When to Use:** Close-ups or portraits of people or animals.

- **How It Works:** Detects and locks focus on the nearest eye, even if the subject moves slightly.

- **Best For:** Shallow depth-of-field portraits where the eyes must be razor-sharp.

Pro Tip: Works brilliantly for vlogging or interviews when you want to maintain sharp focus on the speaker.

How to Track Moving Subjects (Kids, Pets,

Sports)

Tracking movement is where the Canon 90D's autofocus shines—if you set it up correctly.

1. **Switch to AI Servo AF**

   o Mode Dial can stay on Av, Tv, or Manual; the important part is selecting AI Servo in AF settings.

2. **Select Zone AF or Large Zone AF**

   o This gives the camera more area to work with while tracking.

   o For fast-moving subjects, Large Zone AF is more forgiving if your framing isn't perfect.

3. **Use Continuous Shooting Drive Mode**

   o Hold down the shutter to capture a burst of shots—your chances of nailing sharp focus increase.

4. **Keep the Subject in the Frame**

   o The AF system needs to "see" the subject; try to track them smoothly with your movements.

5. **Anticipate the Action**

  o   Start tracking *before* the action peaks (e.g., as the player approaches the goal).

AF Method Cheat Sheet for Quick Decision-Making

Here's a mental shortcut you can memorize:

Situation	AF Mode	AF Method	Drive Mode
Portrait of a person	One-Shot	Face + Tracking	Single Shot
Child running toward you	AI Servo	Large Zone AF	Continuous High
Pet playing	AI Servo	Zone AF	Continuous

fetch			High
Group at a party	One-Shot	Face + Tracking	Single Shot
Bird in flight	AI Servo	Spot AF or Large Zone AF	Continuous High
Selfie/Vlogging	Movie Mode + Eye Detection	Face + Tracking	Continuous

Extra Sharpness Boosters

Even with perfect focus, these small habits make a big difference:

- **Half-Press, Then Shoot:** Let the focus confirm before pressing fully in One-Shot mode.

- **Use a Faster Shutter Speed:** For moving subjects, 1/500 sec or faster works well.

- **Stabilize Your Stance:** Tuck elbows in, use a monopod or tripod if possible.

- **Check Your Lens:** Make sure the image stabilization switch (IS) is on when shooting handheld.

Bottom Line:

Blurry photos aren't a sign that you're bad at photography—they're a sign that your focus settings and shooting technique need to work together. Once you match the AF mode to the subject's behavior and learn to anticipate movement, your 90D will reward you with crisp, sharp images time after time.

When to Use One-Shot AF:

- Portraits
- Landscapes
- Still objects

When to Use AI Servo AF:

- Kids playing
- Pets running
- Sports

Eye Detection AF:

- Close-ups of people &
- animals (portraits)

How to Track Moving Subjects:

- Switch to AI Servo AF
- Select Zone AF or
- Use continuous shooting
- Keep the subject in the frame
- Anticipate the action

Chapter 4

No More Bad Low-Light Shots

Few things are more discouraging than capturing a beautiful moment—your grandchild's school performance, a friend's birthday dinner, a stunning cityscape at night—only to find the photos grainy, blurry, or so dark you can barely see the details. Low-light situations, whether indoors or at night, are one of the trickiest challenges in photography.

The good news is this: the Canon EOS 90D is a powerful camera that can deliver sharp, well-lit images even in dim conditions—if you give it the right instructions. In this chapter, we'll break down why low-light shots go wrong, how to fix them with simple adjustments, how to use natural light to your advantage, and which quick "rescue settings" will help you nail the shot at events, concerts, or night streets.

Why Low-Light Shooting Is Tricky

Photography is all about light—when there's less of it, your camera has to make up the difference in one of three ways:

1. **Increase ISO** (makes the camera's sensor more sensitive to light).

2. **Widen the aperture** (lets more light through the lens).

3. **Slow down the shutter speed** (keeps the shutter open longer to gather more light).

The problem? Each of these has side effects:

- Higher ISO can create grainy noise in the photo.

- Wider aperture reduces depth of field, meaning less of the image is in focus.

- Slower shutter speed can cause motion blur if the subject or your hands move.

Your goal is to balance these three settings so you get enough light without sacrificing sharpness.

Step 1: Simple ISO Adjustments

ISO is your first line of defense in low light.

- For indoor family gatherings: ISO 800–1600 usually works well.

- For concerts or dimly lit events: ISO 3200–6400 might be necessary.

- For night streets with little movement: You can keep ISO lower (800–1600) if you use a tripod.

Pro Tip: *The EOS 90D handles ISO up to 3200 very well for everyday shots. At 6400 and above, expect some noise, but it's often worth it to capture the moment.*

Step 2: Adjust Aperture (f-stop)

The lower the f-number, the wider the aperture, and the more light your lens lets in.

- For portraits in low light: f/2.8–f/4 gives a bright image and nice background blur.

- For group shots where you want more of the scene in focus: f/5.6–f/8.

- Always match the aperture to your subject: if you want sharp focus across the frame, keep it smaller; for artistic blur and more light, go wider.

Pro Tip: *If you only have the kit lens (18–55mm f/3.5–5.6), zoom out to the widest angle to get the lowest f-number.*

Step 3: Control Shutter Speed

The slower the shutter, the more light hits the sensor—but also the more motion blur you risk.

- For still subjects: Try 1/60 sec or slower (use image stabilization and hold steady).

- For moving subjects: Stick to 1/125 sec or faster to freeze motion.

- If using a tripod: You can go as slow as you need (even several seconds) for cityscapes and night scenes.

Pro Tip: *Use the camera's shutter speed priority (Tv) mode if you want to control motion and let the camera handle the rest.*

Using Natural Light to Your Advantage

Before you dive into extreme settings, see if you can improve the light naturally:

- **Move closer to a window** for indoor shots during the day.

- **Position your subject under existing lights**—lamps, streetlights, stage lighting.

- **Avoid mixed light sources** (like a window and tungsten bulbs) to keep colors consistent.

- For candlelight or ambient light scenes, keep your subject close to the light source for warmth and sharpness.

Pro Tip: Turn off overhead fluorescent lights when possible—they can cause unflattering colors and flicker in photos.

Low-Light Rescue Settings

Here are quick setting suggestions you can dial in for common low-light scenarios without guessing:

1. Events & Parties (Handheld)

- Mode: Av (Aperture Priority)
- Aperture: f/2.8–f/4
- ISO: 1600–3200
- Shutter speed safety: 1/60 sec or faster
- White Balance: Auto or set to the room's lighting

2. Concerts or Stage Performances

- Mode: Manual (M) or Tv (Shutter Priority)

- Shutter: 1/125 sec

- Aperture: f/2.8–f/4

- ISO: 3200–6400

- Use Spot Metering to expose for the performer

3. Night Street Photography

- Mode: Manual (M)

- Aperture: f/4–f/8 (for more depth of field)

- Shutter: 1/30 sec handheld, slower with tripod

- ISO: 800–1600 (or higher if handheld)

- Use a tripod whenever possible for maximum sharpness

Extra Low-Light Tips

- **Enable Image Stabilization** on your lens.

- **Shoot in RAW** if you plan to edit—gives you more flexibility to brighten shadows later.

- **Use burst mode** and take several shots—at least one will be tack sharp.

- **Focus manually** in extremely dark scenes where AF struggles.

- **Leverage the viewfinder** instead of Live View to reduce shake when holding the camera.

Bottom Line:

Low-light photography is about knowing how to make light work for you, even when there's very little of it. Once you understand how ISO, aperture, and shutter speed work together—and how to position your subject in the best possible available light—you'll be able to capture crisp, beautiful images long after the sun has set or in the dimmest indoor settings.

LOW-LIGHT RESCUE GUIDE

ISO 3200	
APERTURE (F-STOP) f/2,8	
SHUTTER SPEED 1/60 SEC	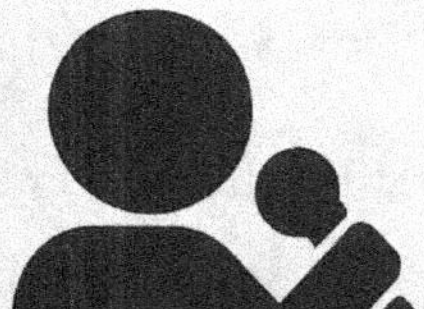

EVENTS & PARTIES

 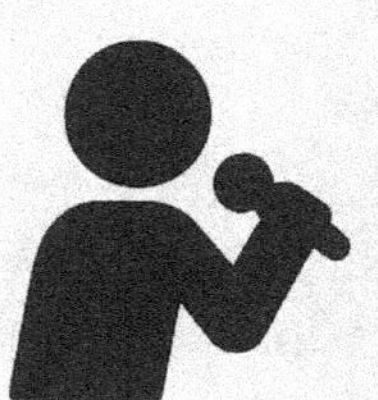 

NIGHT STREETS

USG NATURAL LIG	VATUR

Chapter 5

Video Without the Confusion

If you've bought the Canon EOS 90D partly for its video capabilities, you're not alone. The 90D is a favorite among YouTubers, vloggers, interviewers, and content creators because it can shoot crisp 4K video without a crop (when set correctly), as well as smooth Full HD slow motion for creative shots.

The problem? Many new owners open the video menu and feel lost. There are options for resolution, frame rate, compression type, autofocus settings — and if you don't understand them, you can end up with jittery, cropped, or poor-sounding footage.

This chapter will give you clear, real-world settings for popular video uses, explain how to avoid the dreaded 4K crop, guide you through the best microphone and tripod setups, and give you a quick checklist so you're ready before you hit record.

Easy 4K and Full HD Settings for Common Scenarios

The 90D can shoot:

- **4K Ultra HD** (3840x2160) — best for maximum sharpness.

- **Full HD** (1920x1080) — perfect for everyday use, smaller file sizes, and slow motion.

Here's how to set each scenario:

1. YouTube Videos

- **Resolution:** 4K (3840x2160)

- **Frame Rate:** 30fps (for standard smoothness) or 24fps (for a cinematic feel).

- **Movie Cropping: Disable** to avoid narrowing your field of view.

- **Compression:** IPB (smaller files, easier to edit for beginners).

- **Autofocus:** Movie Servo AF *On* + Face + Tracking.

- *Tip: Use a tripod and an external mic for the best quality.*

2. Interviews

- **Resolution:** Full HD (1920x1080) — still very sharp and easier on storage.

- **Frame Rate:** 30fps for natural movement.

- **Compression:** IPB.

- **Autofocus:** Face + Tracking with Eye Detection ON.

- *Tip: Position the camera at eye level, use a lavalier microphone for clear voice capture, and frame with space above the subject's head.*

3. Slow Motion

- **Resolution:** Full HD (1920x1080).

- **Frame Rate:** 120fps.

- **Compression:** IPB.

- **Autofocus:** Manual focus recommended for consistent results.

- *Tip:* Use this for action, water splashes, sports moves, or dramatic moments. Remember, slow motion needs more light for best results.

How to Avoid Crop Issues in 4K

One of the Canon EOS 90D's best features is that it can shoot uncropped 4K video — but only if you turn off movie cropping in the menu.

To avoid crop:

1. Switch to movie mode (lever near the viewfinder).

2. Press Menu → go to the Movie Recording Quality section.

3. Set Movie Cropping to Disable.

4. Choose your desired resolution and frame rate.

Why this matters:

With movie cropping enabled, your lens's field of view is reduced — for example, a 24mm lens will act more like a 38mm lens, making it harder to fit wide scenes into the frame.

Best Microphone and Tripod Setups for Stable, Clear Videos

Microphones

The built-in microphone is okay for casual clips, but for professional-sounding videos:

- **Lavalier Mic (Clip-On)** — Great for interviews, talking-head YouTube videos.

- **Shotgun Mic** — Mounts on the camera's hot shoe; ideal for vlogs and run-and-gun shooting.

- **USB/Studio Mic** — For voiceovers recorded separately.

Pro Tip: *Always plug into the mic input on the left side of the 90D and set sound recording to* Manual *so you can adjust levels.*

Tripods & Supports

- **Standard Tripod** — Best for interviews and stationary filming.

- **Gorillapod or Mini Tripod** — Flexible legs for table setups and vlogging.

- **Gimbal Stabilizer** — For buttery-smooth walking shots.

Pro Tip: *For handheld shooting, keep your elbows tucked in and enable Movie Digital IS for added stabilization.*

Quick Video Checklist Before Hitting Record

Before you start filming, run through this short checklist to avoid common mistakes:

1. **Battery Charged & Spare Ready** — Video drains power faster than photos.

2. **Memory Card Space** — Use fast SD cards (UHS-I or UHS-II, Class 10 or higher).

3. **Correct Resolution & Frame Rate** — Double-check settings match your purpose.

4. **Focus Mode Set** — Face Tracking ON for people, manual focus for tricky low-light or close-up work.

5. **Stabilization ON** — If handheld.

6. **External Mic Plugged In & Tested** — Do a quick sound check.

7. **Lighting Checked** — Natural light, softbox, or LED panels if indoors.

8. **Framing & Composition** — Keep headroom and straight horizons.

9. **White Balance** — Auto is fine, but lock it for consistent color in longer shoots.

10. **Press Record & Monitor** — Watch the screen or flip-out LCD to ensure everything stays in focus.

Bottom Line:

Video on the Canon EOS 90D doesn't have to be complicated. By choosing the right resolution and frame rate for your project, disabling crop for wider 4K, using a good microphone and stable support, and running through your checklist, you'll get sharp, clear, and professional-looking footage every time.

VIDEO WITHOUT THE CONFUSION

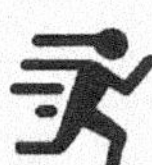 **4K 4K YouTube Videos**

- Resolution: 4K 30fps
- Movie Cropping: Disable
- Autofocus: Face + Tracking

Interviews

- Resolution: Full HD 30fps
- Autofocus: Eye Detection
- Lavalier Mic

AVOIDE CROP ISSUES IN 4

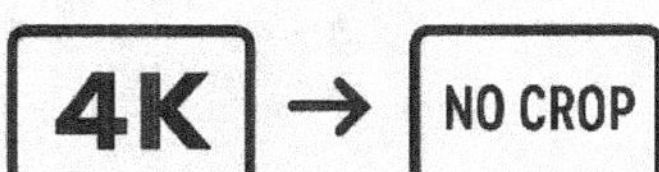

Movie Cropping

Slow Motion

- Resolution: Full HD 120fps
- Autofocus: Manual Focus

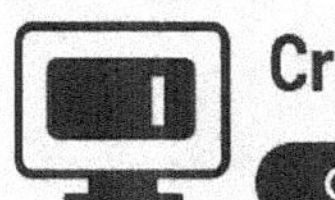 **Crap Issues**

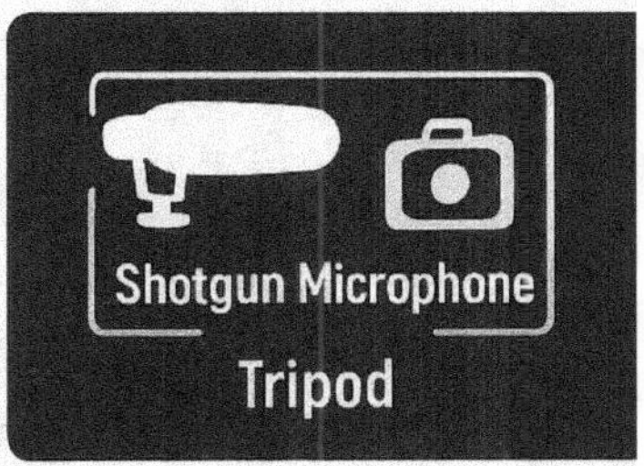

QUICK VIDEO CHECKLIST

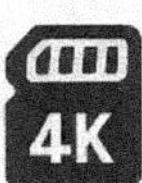

- Battery Charged
- Memory Card Space
- Resolution & Frame Rate
- Autofocus Set

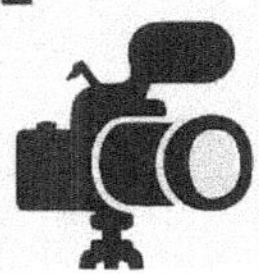

- Stabilization On
- External Mic Plugged In
- Lighting Checked
- Press Record & Monitor

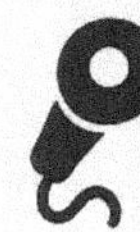

Part 3: Making The Most Of Your 90D's Features

Chapter 6

Mastering Autofocus Like a Pro

The Canon EOS 90D's autofocus system is one of its greatest strengths — fast, accurate, and adaptable. Powered by Canon's Dual Pixel CMOS AF technology, it gives you professional-level control over where and how your camera focuses, whether you're shooting still photos, recording 4K video, or tracking unpredictable subjects.

But here's the truth: many photographers never go beyond the default settings. They leave all focus decisions to the camera, which works fine... until it doesn't. If you've ever had the camera focus on the background instead of your subject, or struggled to keep moving subjects sharp, you've felt the limits of letting the system run on autopilot.

This chapter will show you how Dual Pixel AF works, when to take control and move focus points manually, how to set up Back Button

Focus for faster and sharper results, and how to apply all of this in real-world situations like portraits, wildlife, and action sports.

How Dual Pixel AF Works in Photos and Videos

In most cameras, the pixels on the image sensor either gather light *or* help with focus. In the 90D, every single pixel does both. This is the magic of Dual Pixel CMOS AF — it splits each pixel into two halves that work together to measure focus directly from the image sensor.

Why this matters:

- **In Photos:** You get faster, more accurate focusing in Live View, even in low light.

- **In Video:** You get smooth, natural focus transitions without the "hunting" you see on older systems.

- **In Tracking:** It can follow faces, eyes, or objects across the frame with precision.

When you're using the viewfinder, the 90D relies on a 45-point all cross-type AF system, which is excellent for fast action and stills. Switch to Live View or video mode, and you unlock the full power of Dual Pixel AF across most of the frame.

When to Switch AF Points Manually

Letting the camera choose your AF point works well for general shooting, but there are times when manual point selection is the difference between a keeper and a throwaway.

Switch manually when:

1. **Your subject is off-center**
   - Example: Portrait with the subject on the left side of the frame.
   - Benefit: Keeps your composition intact without having to focus and recompose.

2. **You want precise control in macro or product shots**

o   Example: Photographing a flower's stamen or a piece of jewelry.

o   Benefit: Locks focus exactly where you want detail.

3. **You're shooting through obstacles**

o   Example: Wildlife behind branches or a player behind a net.

o   Benefit: Avoids the camera grabbing focus on the foreground.

How to switch quickly:

- Use the multi-controller joystick on the back to move the AF point.

- In Live View, tap the LCD where you want the focus to lock.

How to Use Back Button Focus for Sharper

Shots

Back Button Focus (BBF) is a game-changer for many photographers. It separates focusing from the shutter button, giving you more control.

Why it works:

- Eliminates accidental refocusing when you press the shutter.
- Lets you switch between continuous and single focus instantly without changing settings.
- Perfect for sports, wildlife, and any situation where subjects move unpredictably.

How to set it up:

1. Press Menu.
2. Go to the Custom Functions section.
3. Find Shutter/AF-ON Button Settings.

4. Set the shutter button to "Metering only" and assign autofocus to the AF-ON button on the back.

5. Now, press AF-ON to focus; press the shutter only to take the shot.

Using BBF in practice:

- Hold AF-ON to track moving subjects in AI Servo.

- Release AF-ON to lock focus on a still subject and recompose without losing focus.

Real-Life AF Case Studies

Portraits

- **AF Mode:** One-Shot AF.

- **AF Method:** Face + Tracking with Eye Detection ON.

- **Tip:** For shallow depth of field (e.g., f/2.8), Eye Detection ensures the eyes — not the nose or ears — are the sharpest point.

Wildlife

- **AF Mode:** AI Servo AF.

- **AF Method:** Zone AF or Large Zone AF.

- **Tip:** Use Back Button Focus to track an animal that might pause, move, then pause again. Keep the AF point over the head or upper body.

Action Sports

- **AF Mode:** AI Servo AF.

- **AF Method:** Large Zone AF for erratic motion; Spot AF for predictable paths.

- **Tip:** Start tracking the athlete before the key moment so the system locks on and anticipates movement.

Extra Pro Tips for Nailing Focus

- **Use the Right Drive Mode:** Continuous shooting increases your chances of getting a perfectly focused frame in a burst.

- **Mind Your Shutter Speed:** Even perfect focus can't save motion blur from a too-slow shutter.

- **Combine AF with Stabilization:** On longer lenses, image stabilization reduces camera shake so your AF work pays off.

Bottom Line:

Mastering autofocus on the Canon EOS 90D is about knowing when to trust the camera and when to take control. By understanding how Dual Pixel AF works, learning to move AF points manually, using Back Button Focus, and applying the right settings in real-world scenarios, you'll consistently get sharper, more accurate shots — no matter the subject or speed.

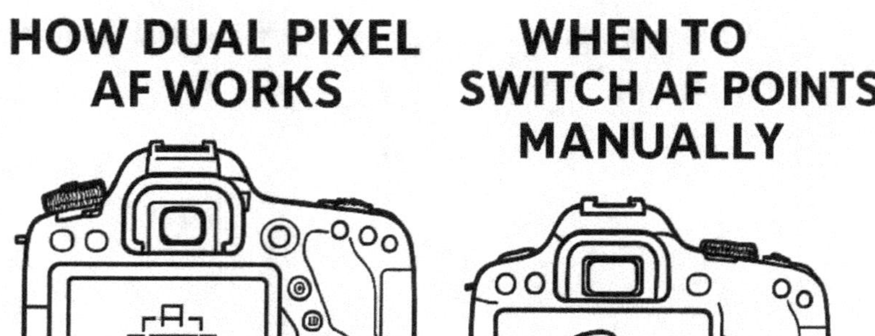

Chapter 7

Creative Photography Made Easy

Technical skills will help you get a sharp, well-exposed shot — but creativity is what turns that shot into something memorable. The Canon EOS 90D has the tools to help you create photographs that stand out, but those tools are most powerful when you combine them with a good eye for composition and a playful, experimental mindset.

In this chapter, we'll strip away the intimidation around "artistic" photography. You'll learn simple composition techniques that work in any situation, discover how to use your 90D's Picture Styles to add personality to your shots, explore fun challenges to sharpen your eye, and try a practical exercise in visual storytelling.

Composition Basics: The Three Rules That

Transform Your Shots

The arrangement of elements within your frame is often the difference between a snapshot and a striking image. These three techniques will instantly make your photos more engaging:

1. Rule of Thirds

Imagine your frame divided into a grid of nine equal rectangles — two equally spaced vertical lines and two equally spaced horizontal lines. Placing your subject along one of these lines, or at the intersections, creates balance and draws the viewer's eye naturally.

- **Portraits:** Place the subject's eyes along the upper third line.

- **Landscapes:** Position the horizon along either the top or bottom third.

- **Tip:** Turn on the grid display in your EOS 90D (*Menu → Shooting Settings → Grid Display ON*) to help with framing.

2. Leading Lines

Lines in your scene — a road, fence, riverbank, row of trees — can guide the viewer's eye toward your subject.

- **Use in travel shots:** Roads leading into mountains.

- **Use in portraits:** A pathway or railing drawing attention toward the person.

- **Tip:** Position lines so they start from the edges of your frame and point inward.

3. Framing

Look for natural elements to "frame" your subject — windows, doorways, archways, overhanging branches.

- **Why it works:** Framing focuses attention and adds depth.

- **Tip:** Move slightly to position the frame perfectly around your subject without distractions.

How to Use Picture Styles for Creative Effects

Your Canon EOS 90D's Picture Styles change the color, contrast, and sharpness of your images in-camera — giving you a head start on creative looks without editing software.

Popular Picture Styles:

- **Standard:** Balanced, all-purpose.

- **Portrait:** Softer skin tones, smoother detail.

- **Landscape:** Boosted blues and greens, more sharpness.

- **Monochrome:** Black-and-white photography straight out of the camera.

- **Neutral/Faithful:** Flat tones for later editing.

How to Change Picture Style:

1. Press the **Q button**.

2. Highlight **Picture Style**.

3. Scroll to choose your desired style.

Pro Tip: *You can customize each style — increasing contrast for drama, lowering saturation for a muted look — then save it for future use.*

Fun Photography Challenges to Build Skill

Sometimes the best way to grow creatively is to give yourself constraints. These mini-challenges are designed to get you out shooting with purpose.

1. **Color Hunt:** Spend a day photographing only one color — red doors, red cars, red jackets.

2. **One Lens Only:** Choose one lens and shoot everything with it, forcing you to move and rethink your angles.

3. **Silhouette Day:** Shoot only against strong backlight to capture dark, dramatic outlines.

4. **Texture Focus:** Photograph surfaces — wood grain, peeling paint, rippling water — filling the frame.

5. **50 Steps Rule:** Wherever you start, walk exactly 50 steps and take a photo from that spot.

These challenges train your eye to notice patterns, colors, and details you might otherwise miss.

Example: Capturing a Story in 3 Images

Photography isn't just about single shots — it can also tell a story through a sequence. Here's how to create a simple 3-photo narrative:

1. Establishing Shot (The Setting)

- Wide shot that shows the environment.
- Example: A quiet park with morning light spilling through trees.

2. Medium Shot (The Subject)

- Focus on your main subject in context.
- Example: A jogger stretching beside a bench.

3. Close-Up (The Detail)

- A tight shot that adds emotion or texture.

- Example: The jogger's shoes on the path, laces slightly undone.

Pro Tip: Think like a filmmaker — wide, medium, close-up — to draw viewers into your scene.

Bringing It All Together

Composition rules, creative camera settings, and playful challenges are like exercises for your visual muscles. By practicing them regularly, you'll start seeing potential photographs everywhere. Soon, you won't have to think about the Rule of Thirds or leading lines — they'll become instinctive, and your images will have more depth, mood, and impact.

CREATIVE PHOTOGRAPHY MADE EASY

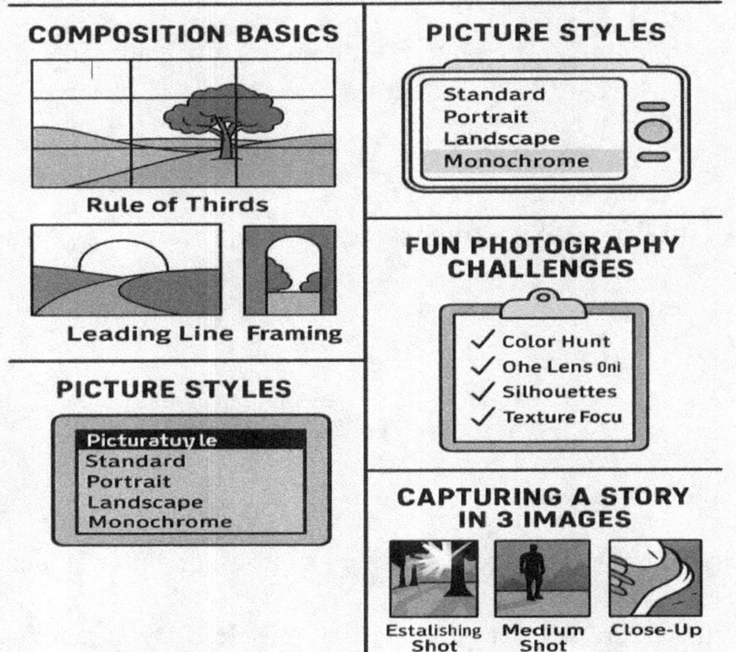

Chapter 8

Picking the Right Lens for the Job

A camera body is only half the equation when it comes to great photography. The other half — and arguably the more important — is the lens you attach to it. Your lens determines not only how much of the scene you capture but also how sharp, bright, and creatively expressive your images can be.

The Canon EOS 90D can use a huge variety of lenses, from compact primes to long telephotos. But with so many options, how do you know which one to use for portraits, travel, sports, or wildlife? In this chapter, we'll break down focal lengths in plain English, recommend the best lenses for popular photography styles, and give you affordable upgrade options that will dramatically improve your results without draining your budget.

Understanding Focal Lengths in Simple Terms

Focal length is measured in millimeters (mm) and is printed on your lens (e.g., 18–55mm or 50mm). It affects two main things:

1. **How much of the scene you see (field of view)**

   - Short focal lengths (wide-angle) show more of the scene.

   - Long focal lengths (telephoto) zoom in on distant subjects.

2. **How the image looks (perspective and background blur)**

   - Wide-angle lenses exaggerate depth and keep more in focus.

   - Telephoto lenses compress the scene and blur the background more.

On the EOS 90D's APS-C sensor, you also need to remember the 1.6x crop factor:

- A 50mm lens acts more like an 80mm lens in terms of field of view.

- A 100mm lens behaves like a 160mm.

Recommended Lenses by Photography Style

1. Portraits

- **Ideal Focal Length:** 50mm to 85mm (on full-frame), which means around 35mm to 50mm for APS-C, or 50mm to 85mm actual lenses if you want more compression.

- **Why:** Creates flattering facial proportions and a soft, blurred background.

- **Popular Choices:**

  - Canon EF 50mm f/1.8 STM (light, affordable, excellent in low light).

  - Canon EF-S 60mm f/2.8 Macro USM (also works for close-up details).

2. Travel

- **Ideal Focal Length:** 18–135mm (a flexible zoom range).

- **Why:** Versatile enough for landscapes, street shots, and occasional close-ups without changing lenses.

- **Popular Choices:**

  - Canon EF-S 18–135mm f/3.5–5.6 IS USM (sharp, lightweight, and has image stabilization).

  - Canon EF-S 15–85mm f/3.5–5.6 IS USM (wider at the short end for big cityscapes).

3. Sports

- **Ideal Focal Length:** 70–200mm or longer.

- **Why:** Lets you fill the frame with action from a distance.

- **Popular Choices:**

  - Canon EF 70–200mm f/4L USM (sharp, fast focusing).

  - Canon EF 70–300mm f/4–5.6 IS II USM (budget-friendly, good reach).

4. Wildlife

- **Ideal Focal Length:** 300mm or more.

- **Why:** Gets you close to distant animals without disturbing them.

- **Popular Choices:**

  - Canon EF 100–400mm f/4.5–5.6L IS II USM (professional-grade, stunning quality).

  - Canon EF 400mm f/5.6L USM (lightweight prime for serious birders).

  - Sigma/Tamron 150–600mm lenses (third-party super-zooms at competitive prices).

Affordable Lens Upgrades for Beginners

If you're currently using the standard kit lens (usually an EF-S 18–55mm), you've already got a capable all-rounder. But adding even one of these affordable upgrades can open up new possibilities:

1. **Canon EF 50mm f/1.8 STM ("Nifty Fifty")**

o   Inexpensive, sharp, and excellent in low light.

o   Great for portraits, indoor events, and shallow depth-of-field shots.

2. **Canon EF-S 24mm f/2.8 STM (Pancake Lens)**

o   Ultra-compact, wide enough for travel and street photography.

o   Makes your 90D lighter and less intimidating for candid shooting.

3. **Canon EF-S 55–250mm f/4–5.6 IS STM**

o   Affordable telephoto option for sports, wildlife, and distant landscapes.

o   Image stabilization helps keep shots sharp at longer focal lengths.

4. **Third-Party Options** (Sigma, Tamron, Tokina)

o   Often cheaper than Canon lenses with similar performance.

o   Check for EF or EF-S mounts to ensure compatibility.

Matching Lenses to Your Photography Goals

- If you want beautiful portraits → Start with a fast prime (50mm f/1.8).

- If you want to travel light but be ready for anything → Get a versatile zoom (18–135mm).

- If you want sports or wildlife reach → Choose a telephoto zoom (70–300mm or longer).

- If you want to experiment creatively → Try a macro lens or a wide prime for new perspectives.

Bottom Line:

The right lens isn't always the most expensive — it's the one that helps you capture the kinds of images you love to shoot. Start with what you have, then add lenses that expand your capabilities in the areas that matter most to you. Over time, you'll build a lens kit that works perfectly for your style and your Canon EOS 90D.

Picking the Right Lens for the Job

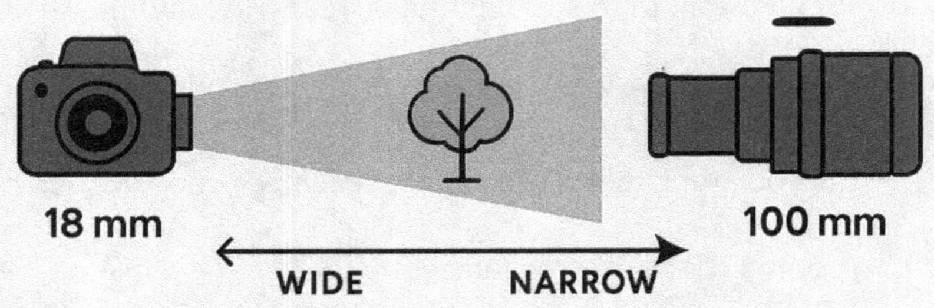

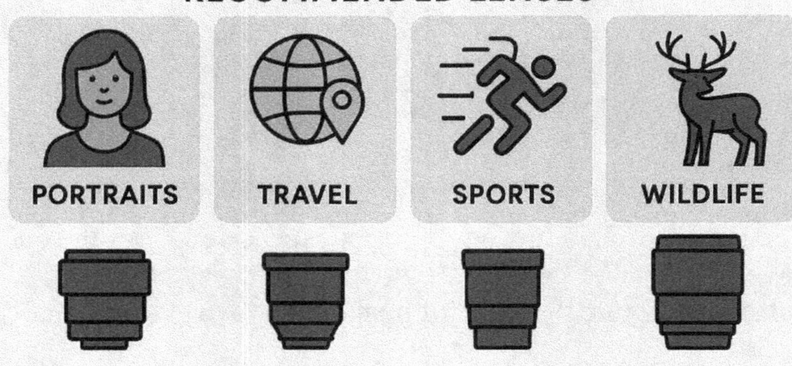

AFFORDABLE LENS UPGRADES

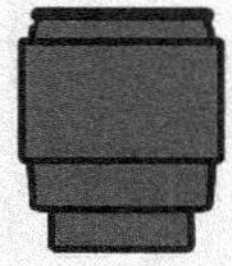

Affordable Lens Upgrades

Part 4: Practical Camera Care & Efficiency

Chapter 9

Memory Cards, Storage & Backup Made Simple

If your Canon EOS 90D is the brain, your memory card is its memory bank. It's where every photo and video you shoot lives—at least until you transfer or back it up. Many photographers spend hours learning exposure settings, but neglect one of the most important parts of the process: safe, reliable storage.

In this chapter, we'll keep things straightforward and cover which SD cards work best for your 90D, how to avoid "Card Full" and lost files, and a simple, repeatable backup process so you can sleep easy knowing your work is safe.

Best SD Cards for Speed and Reliability

The EOS 90D supports UHS-II SD cards for faster read/write speeds, but will also work with UHS-I cards. The difference is most noticeable when shooting high-speed bursts or recording high-resolution 4K video.

Key features to look for:

- **Capacity:** 64GB is a sweet spot for most users. 128GB if you shoot long videos or RAW stills often.
- **Speed Class:**
    - For still photography: UHS-I, Class 10 or higher.
    - For 4K video: UHS-I or UHS-II with a Video Speed Class rating of V30 or higher.
- **Brand reliability:** Stick with known brands like SanDisk, Lexar, Sony, or Kingston.

Example choices:

- **Budget-friendly:** SanDisk Extreme 64GB UHS-I V30

- **Faster option:** Lexar Professional 2000x 64GB UHS-II

- **Video-heavy shooters:** Sony Tough Series 64GB UHS-II (extra durable and water-resistant)

How to Avoid "Card Full" and Lost Files

A memory card error or full card in the middle of a shoot is frustrating, but it's preventable.

Tips to prevent it:

1. **Format your card in-camera before each new shoot**

   This clears old data properly and keeps the card healthy.

2. **Don't delete photos one by one from the camera**

   This can cause file fragmentation. Wait until you can transfer them to a computer.

3. **Carry a spare card**

   Keep it in a small waterproof case in your bag or pocket.

4. **Watch your space during shoots**

   Press the "Info" button to check remaining shots or video time.

5. **Avoid using the same card in multiple camera brands**

   This can cause file system conflicts and potential corruption.

Step-by-Step Backup Workflow After a Shoot

The safest photographers follow the 3-2-1 backup rule:

- 3 copies of your files

- 2 different types of storage (e.g., hard drive + cloud)

- 1 copy off-site in case of disaster

Here's a simple backup process for 90D users:

Step 1 – Transfer immediately

- Use a card reader for faster transfers instead of plugging the camera directly into the computer.

- Copy files to a dedicated folder labeled with the date and shoot name.

Step 2 – Primary storage

- Save the files to your main computer or an external hard drive.

- Organize by year → month → shoot name for quick retrieval.

Step 3 – Secondary backup

- Use a second external drive or network-attached storage (NAS).

- Alternatively, upload to a cloud service (Google Drive, Dropbox, Backblaze, or Amazon Photos).

Step 4 – Verify before formatting

- Open a few random images and videos to ensure they transferred properly.

- Only then should you format the card in-camera for the next shoot.

Pro Tips for Long-Term File Safety

- **Label your cards** with a marker or sticker for quick identification.

- **Replace cards every 2–3 years** if you shoot often—flash memory wears out.

- **Keep cards in a padded case** to protect from dust, water, and bending.

- **Don't fill a card completely**—leave a small buffer to avoid write errors.

Bottom Line:

Your camera is only as reliable as the memory card and backup habits you use. By choosing high-quality SD cards, keeping them healthy, and following a simple backup workflow, you'll protect your images from one of the most heartbreaking experiences a

photographer can face—losing irreplaceable memories.

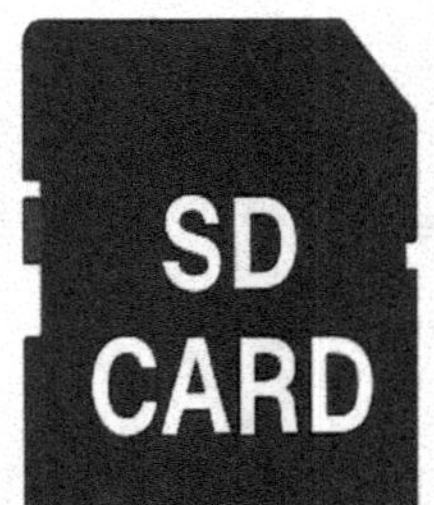

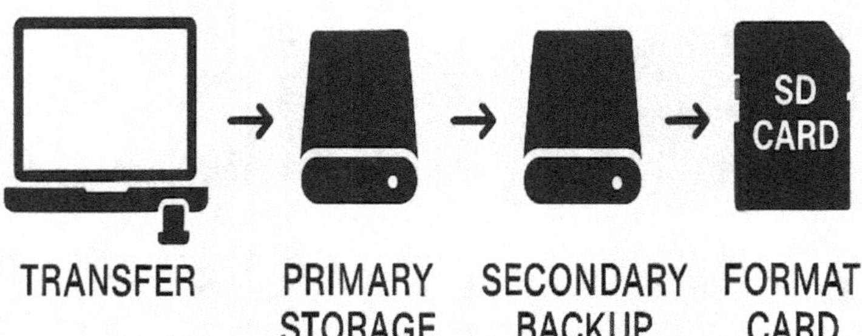

Chapter 10

Getting the Most from Your Battery

The Canon EOS 90D uses the LP-E6N rechargeable lithium-ion battery, a reliable workhorse that has powered many Canon cameras over the years. On paper, it can deliver around 1,300 shots per charge when using the optical viewfinder — but in real-world shooting, especially with video or Live View, many photographers see that number drop dramatically.

This chapter will help you understand why your battery drains faster, how to optimize settings for longer shooting sessions, and which spare battery and charging habits will keep you shooting without interruptions.

Why the Battery Drains Quickly in Video/Live

View

When you shoot through the optical viewfinder, your camera uses minimal power — it's mostly running the light meter and autofocus system. But in Live View or video mode, the camera's LCD screen (or EVF) stays on continuously, the sensor is active the whole time, and autofocus is constantly running.

High drain factors include:

- **4K or high-frame-rate video recording** – processing and writing large files uses more energy.

- **Image stabilization (IS) lenses** – the IS system runs constantly while half-pressing the shutter or recording.

- **Wi-Fi and Bluetooth** – keeping wireless connections active eats battery life.

- **Cold weather** – low temperatures reduce battery efficiency.

Pro Tip: *If you're shooting video for extended periods, expect battery life to be half or less of the CIPA-rated number.*

Power-Saving Menu Tweaks

You don't have to sacrifice convenience for battery life. A few quick adjustments can give you up to 30–40% longer usage without affecting image quality.

1. Enable Auto Power Off

- Menu → Wrench icon → *Auto Power Off* → Set to 1 min or less.

2. Lower Screen Brightness

- Menu → Wrench icon → *LCD Brightness* → Reduce to a comfortable but not maximum level.

3. Turn Off Wireless Functions When Not in Use

- Menu → Wrench icon → *Wireless Communication Settings* → Disable Wi-Fi and Bluetooth unless transferring files.

4. Use the Optical Viewfinder Instead of Live View When Possible

- Especially for still photography — it reduces sensor and LCD use.

5. Limit Image Review Time

- Menu → Playback Settings → *Image Review* → Set to 2 seconds or less.

6. Disable Continuous Sensor Cleaning Between Shots

- Menu → Wrench icon → *Sensor Cleaning* → Set to "Auto (At Power Off)" instead of every startup.

Recommended Spare Battery Options

Nothing beats the peace of mind of having extra fully charged batteries in your bag.

Canon-branded:

- **LP-E6N** – The standard battery supplied with the 90D. Excellent reliability.

- **LP-E6NH** – Slightly higher capacity (2130mAh) and fully compatible.

Third-party options (choose quality brands only):

- Wasabi Power LP-E6N

- Watson LP-E6N

  (Ensure they're fully compatible and have good reviews — cheap, unbranded batteries can fail prematurely or show incorrect charge levels.)

Tip: *If you buy third-party batteries, also get their dedicated charger to avoid charging issues.*

Charging Tips for Longer Battery Life

Lithium-ion batteries like the LP-E6N don't develop a "memory," but they do have a finite charge cycle life. Proper care can keep them performing at their best for years.

1. Avoid Fully Draining Often

- Recharge when your battery hits around 20–30% instead of waiting for it to die.

2. Store Partially Charged if Not in Use

- If you won't use the camera for a while, store batteries at around 50–60% charge in a cool, dry place.

3. Use the Original Canon Charger When Possible

- It provides optimal charging current and temperature control.

4. Don't Charge in Extreme Heat or Cold

- Aim for room temperature for safest charging.

5. Rotate Your Batteries

- If you have multiple, use and charge them in rotation to keep wear even.

Quick Grab-and-Go Checklist for Power Confidence

- Always carry at least one spare battery for casual photography and two or more for all-day events or video work.

- Charge all batteries the night before a shoot.

- Keep spares in a small padded pouch or case to protect from moisture and short-circuits.

- Turn off the camera between setups instead of letting it idle with Live View running.

Bottom Line:

Battery life issues on the Canon EOS 90D are entirely manageable once you know what's causing the drain and how to plan ahead. With the right menu tweaks, smart usage habits, and a couple of well-maintained spares, you can shoot all day without the dreaded red battery icon cutting your session short.

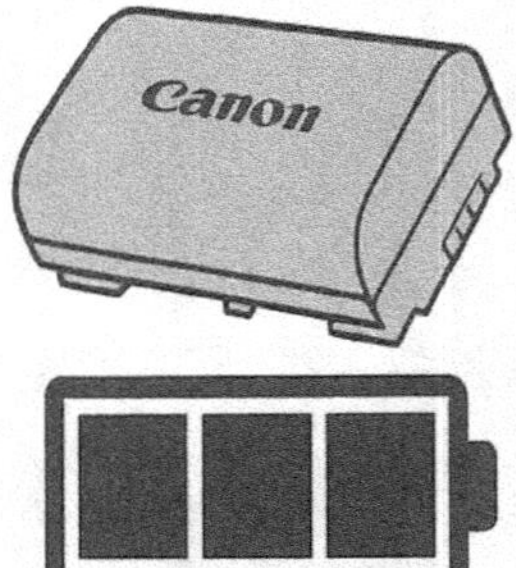

WHY THE BATTERY DRAINS QUICKLY IN VIDEO/LIVE VIEW

- LCD and sensor always on
- Autofocus working continuously
- 4K video recording
- Cold weather

POWER-SAVING MENU TWEAKS

- Enable Auto Power Off
- Lower screen brightness
- Turn off Wi-Fi when not in use
- Limit Image review time

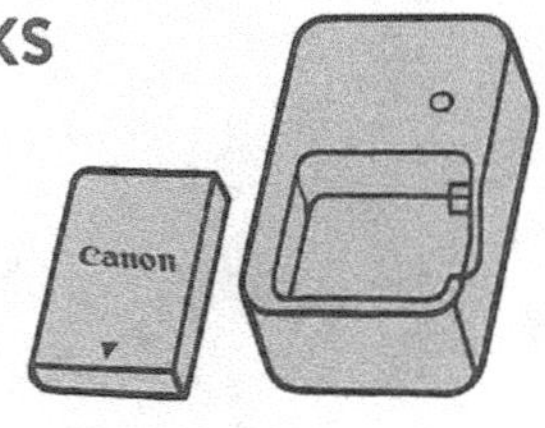

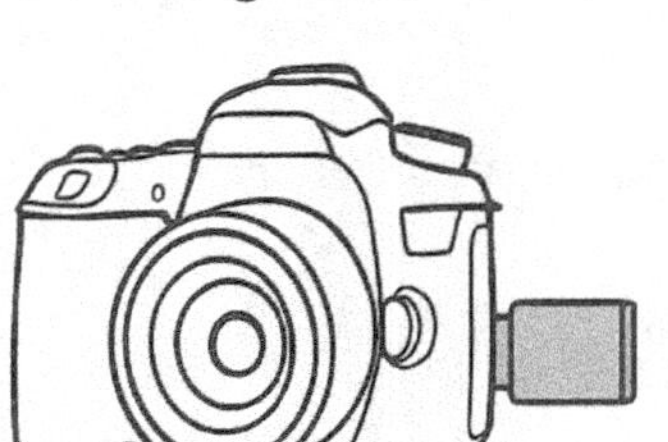

CHARGING TIPS

- Avoid frequent full discharges
- Store partially charged
- Use the Canon charger
- Charge at room temperature

RECOMMENDED SPARE BATTERIES

Chapter 11

Keeping Your Camera in Top Shape

Your Canon EOS 90D is a precision tool — a blend of delicate electronics, fine mechanics, and optical glass. Treat it well, and it will reward you with years of reliable performance. Neglect it, and you could end up with blurry images, malfunctioning buttons, or expensive repair bills. This chapter will show you how to clean, store, and handle your camera in a way that prevents damage and keeps it looking and performing like new.

Cleaning the Lens and Sensor Safely

1. Cleaning the Lens

Your lens is your camera's eye — a dirty lens can ruin a perfect shot. But cleaning it the wrong way can scratch coatings and permanently reduce sharpness.

- **Step 1 – Blow Away Loose Dust**

  Use a hand-squeezed air blower (never canned air — the propellant can damage glass).

- **Step 2 – Brush Gently**

  Use a dedicated lens brush to remove particles without pressing hard.

- **Step 3 – Wipe with a Microfiber Cloth**

  Lightly wipe in circular motions from the center outward. If there are smudges, use a drop of lens cleaning fluid on the cloth — never directly on the lens.

Pro Tip: Keep the lens cap on whenever you're not shooting to reduce the need for frequent cleaning.

2. Cleaning the Sensor

The sensor is the heart of your camera. Dust on the sensor shows up as dark spots in your images, especially at smaller apertures (f/11 and above).

- **Automatic Sensor Cleaning:**

  The EOS 90D has a built-in sensor cleaning feature that vibrates the low-pass filter to shake off dust. Make sure it's enabled in your menu (usually runs at startup or shutdown).

- **Manual Air Blower Cleaning:**

  If dust remains, use a blower with the camera's sensor exposed (Menu → Manual Cleaning Mode). Always hold the camera facing downward so dust falls out, not in.

- **Professional Cleaning:**

  If you still see spots after cleaning, let a Canon service center or reputable camera shop handle a wet clean — doing it yourself without training can cause serious damage.

Storing the Camera for Travel and Long Breaks

A DSLR can survive years of travel if stored properly — but improper storage can lead to fungus, corrosion, and mechanical stiffness.

For Short-Term Travel

- Use a padded camera bag with compartments to protect gear from bumps.

- Keep silica gel packs inside to absorb moisture.

- Avoid leaving the camera in a hot car — heat can warp plastic and damage electronics.

For Long Breaks (weeks or months)

- Remove the battery to prevent leakage or slow discharge.

- Store in a cool, dry place away from direct sunlight.

- Keep the camera inside a dust-proof bag or cabinet.

- Periodically power it on and take a few shots to keep internal lubricants distributed.

Common Mistakes That Damage Cameras (and How to Avoid Them)

1. **Changing Lenses in Dusty or Windy Conditions**

o   *Why it's bad:* Dust can get on the sensor or inside the lens.

o   *Solution:* Change lenses with your camera facing downward and do it quickly.

2. **Wiping a Dry Lens with Your Shirt**

o   *Why it's bad:* Dirt particles can scratch coatings.

o   *Solution:* Always use a clean microfiber cloth.

3. **Carrying the Camera by the Strap Only**

o   *Why it's bad:* Straps can detach unexpectedly.

o   *Solution:* Always hold the camera body securely when walking.

4. **Leaving the Camera in Humid or Damp Environments**

o   *Why it's bad:* Encourages fungus growth inside lenses.

o   *Solution:* Use silica gel and store in a dry place.

5. **Forgetting to Cap the Lens**

o   *Why it's bad:* Dust, fingerprints, and scratches build up.

o   *Solution:* Cap it every time you stop shooting.

Quick Care Routine Checklist

- **After every shoot:** Wipe down the body with a soft, dry cloth.

- **Weekly:** Check lens glass for smudges and clean if needed.

- **Monthly:** Inspect sensor for dust spots.

- **Every 6–12 months:** Get a professional cleaning if you shoot heavily.

Bottom Line:

Taking care of your Canon EOS 90D isn't complicated — it's about preventing problems before they happen. A few minutes of care after each shoot will save you hours of frustration later, and could easily add years to your camera's life.

CLEANING THE LENS AND SENSOR

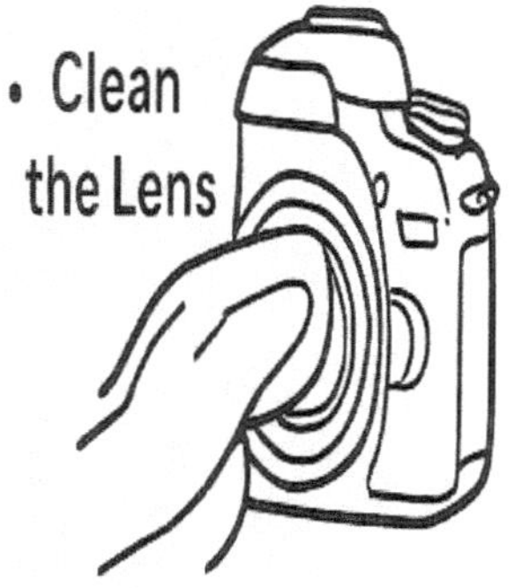

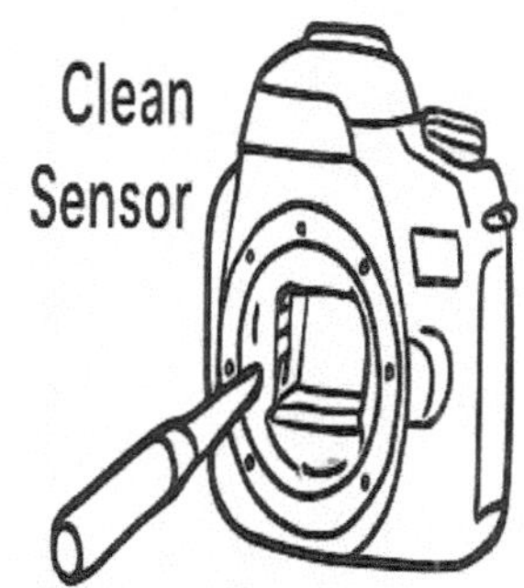

- Use a blower
- Brush and cloth
- If drower

- Use as automatic sensor cleaning fic, ause
- A blower if necessary

STORING THE CAMERA

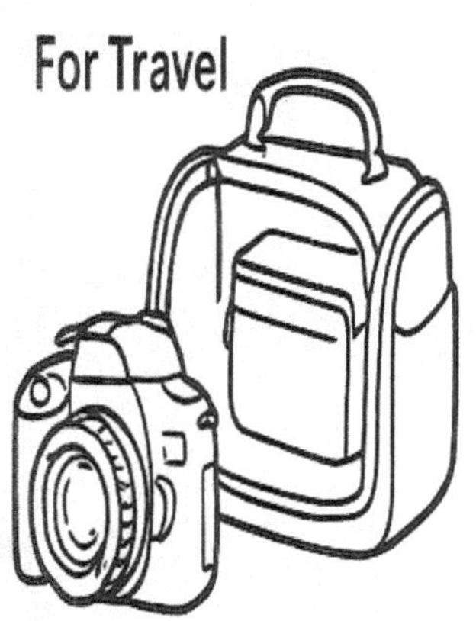

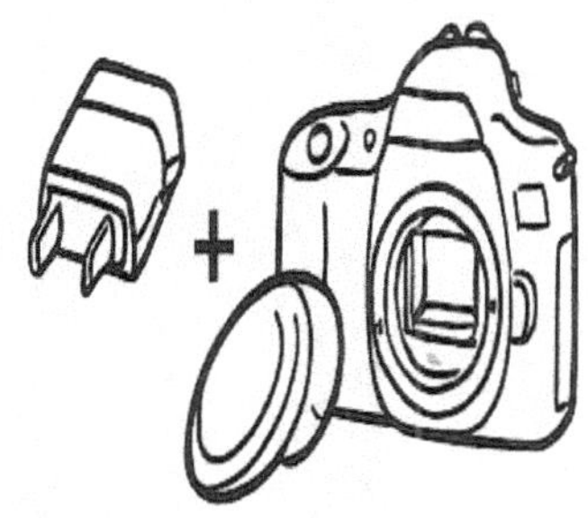

- Store in cam bag

- Remove battery
- Store cam t a dy place

Part 5: Putting It All Together

Chapter 12

Real-World Shooting Scenarios

Reading about camera settings is one thing — using them when life is happening in front of you is another. This chapter will take you into four real-life situations where you can put your Canon EOS 90D to work, with clear, beginner-friendly settings, lens suggestions, and pro tips that ensure you come home with images worth keeping.

Scenario 1: Indoor Birthday Party Setup

Indoor events like birthday parties are full of fast-moving moments — blowing candles, laughter, hugs — but the light is often dim, and flash can be unflattering if used carelessly.

Best Lens:

- A 35mm f/1.8 or 50mm f/1.8 prime lens for low-light capability without flash.

Recommended Settings:

- **Mode:** Aperture Priority (Av)

- **Aperture:** f/2.0–f/2.8 for shallow depth of field and more light.

- **ISO:** Auto, max limit set to 3200 to prevent excessive noise.

- **White Balance:** Auto or adjust to match room lighting.

- **Drive Mode:** Continuous (for capturing multiple expressions quickly).

Tips:

- Stand back and use a slightly longer focal length to capture natural expressions without intruding.

- If using flash, bounce it off the ceiling for softer, more flattering light.

- Capture a mix of candid moments and key posed shots (cake cutting, family group).

Scenario 2: Outdoor Sports/Wildlife Shoot

Whether you're photographing your child's soccer game or a bird in flight, you'll need fast autofocus and a shutter speed that freezes action.

Best Lens:

- Canon EF 70–300mm f/4-5.6 IS USM or EF 100–400mm f/4.5-5.6L IS II USM for reach and sharpness.

Recommended Settings:

- **Mode:** Shutter Priority (Tv)
- **Shutter Speed:** 1/1000 sec for fast sports; 1/2000 sec for birds in flight.
- **ISO:** Auto (may rise to 800–1600 outdoors in cloudy weather).
- **AF Mode:** AI Servo for continuous focus tracking.

- **AF Point Selection:** Zone AF or Single Point (center) for precision.

Tips:

- Pre-focus on an area where the action will happen.

- Use burst mode to increase your chance of capturing the perfect moment.

- For wildlife, stay still and let the subject move into your frame.

Scenario 3: Vacation Vlog

Travel vlogging demands a balance of great visuals, smooth motion, and clear audio. The Canon EOS 90D shines in this area if set up correctly.

Best Lens:

- Canon EF-S 18–135mm IS USM (versatile zoom) or EF-S 10–18mm IS STM (for wide, immersive views).

Recommended Settings:

- **Mode:** Manual for video (so exposure doesn't change mid-shot).

- **Resolution:** 4K at 25/30fps for high detail; 1080p at 60fps for smoother motion.

- **Shutter Speed:** 1/50 sec (for 25fps) or 1/60 sec (for 30fps).

- **Aperture:** f/4–f/5.6 for balanced sharpness and depth.

- **ISO:** Auto with a limit of 1600.

Tips:

- Use an external microphone for better sound.

- Stabilize shots with a small travel tripod or handheld gimbal.

- Record "B-roll" clips (street scenes, food, landscapes) to make your vlog engaging.

Scenario 4: Sunset Portrait Session

Shooting portraits at sunset (golden hour) creates warm, flattering light — but the light fades quickly, so you need to be ready.

Best Lens:

- Canon EF 85mm f/1.8 or EF-S 55–250mm IS STM for beautiful background blur.

Recommended Settings:

- **Mode:** Aperture Priority (Av)
- **Aperture:** f/2.0–f/4 for shallow depth of field and background separation.
- **ISO:** Start at 100, raise as light fades (up to 1600).
- **White Balance:** Daylight for warm tones, or Cloudy for even richer colors.
- **Metering Mode:** Spot or Evaluative, depending on lighting contrast.

Tips:

- Position the subject with the sun behind them for a glowing rim light.

- Use a reflector or fill flash to light the face if it's too shadowed.

- Keep shooting through the fading light — the sky can turn dramatically colorful just after sunset.

Final Word on Real-World Scenarios

The Canon EOS 90D is more than just a technical tool — it's a storyteller. The more you understand which settings to use in each situation, the less you'll have to think about the camera and the more you can focus on capturing memories as they unfold. These scenarios are only starting points; with time, you'll tweak and adapt them to match your style.

REAL-WORLD SHOOTING SCENARIOS

INDOOR BIRTHDAY PARTY

Recommended Settings
Mode: Av (*Apt..*)
Aperture: f/2.8
ISO: *Auto*
Best Lens: 35 mm or 50 mm

- Bounce flash off ceiling

OUTDOOR SPORTS/WILDLIFE

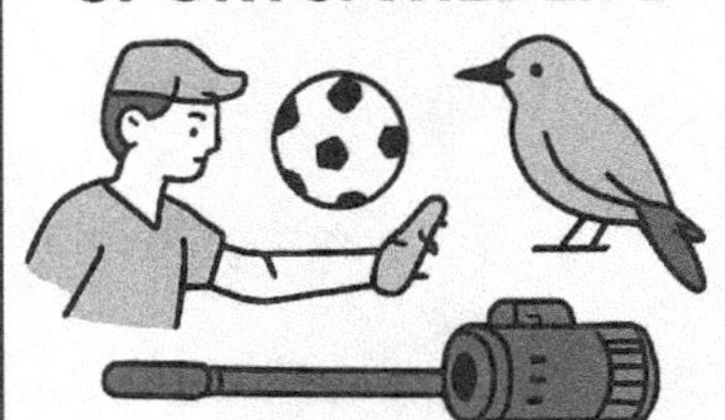

Recommended Settings
Mode: Tv
Shutter-Speed: 1/1000 (spts)
ISO: Auto
Bast Len: 70-300 mm AF

- Use AI Servo AF for tracking

VACATION VLOG

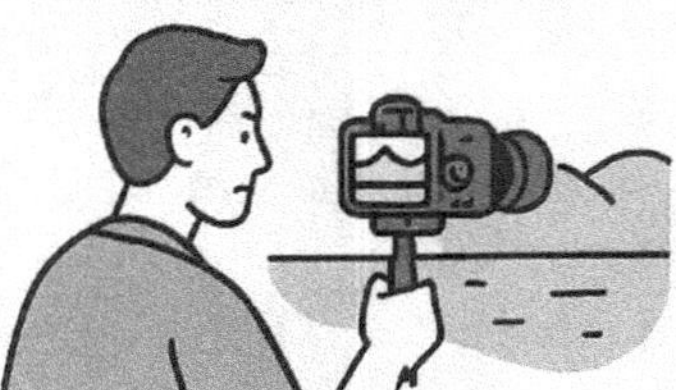

Recommended Settings
Mode: Movie
Resolution: 4K
Shutter Speed: 160
Aperture: f/4

- Use an external microphone

SUNSET PORTRAIT

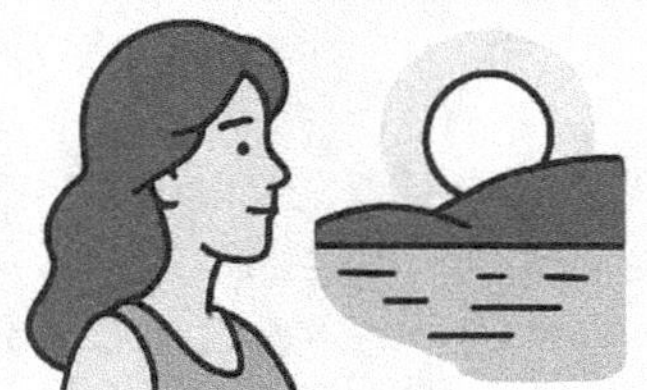

Recommended Settings
Mode: Av
Aperture: f/2.8
ISO limit o 1600 Dayiight
Bast Lens: 85 mm

- Shoot during golden hour

Chapter 13

10-Day Photo & Video Challenge

Learning a camera is a lot like learning a language — the more you use it in real situations, the faster it becomes second nature. This 10-day challenge is designed to help you develop muscle memory, confidence, and a sense of creative fun with your Canon EOS 90D. Each day focuses on one feature or technique you've learned in this book, so by the end, you'll be shooting without second-guessing yourself.

Day 1 – Find Your Perfect Grip

Focus: Steady handholding and basic composition

- Go outside and take five photos of everyday objects — flowers, lampposts, pets — while experimenting with how you hold the camera.

- Keep elbows tucked in, feet shoulder-width apart, and gently press the shutter instead of jabbing it.

- Review your shots on the LCD and note which ones look sharpest.

Day 2 – Master Aperture Priority (Av Mode)

Focus: Depth of field control

- Set the camera to Av mode.

- Take three shots of the same subject (e.g., a coffee mug) at f/2.8, f/5.6, and f/11.

- Compare how the background changes from blurred to detailed.

- Tip: Use a subject with a clear background to see the effect more dramatically.

Day 3 – Freeze the Action

Focus: Shutter Priority (Tv Mode)

- Find a moving subject — kids playing, cars passing, or water from a fountain.

- Start at 1/1000 sec to freeze the action, then drop to 1/60 sec to see motion blur.

- This teaches you how shutter speed affects movement in your photos.

Day 4 – Go Manual with Focus

Focus: Manual Focus and AF point selection

- Photograph an object with distractions in the background.

- Switch to manual focus and fine-tune until the subject is tack-sharp.

- Then try the same shot with a single AF point selected, and notice the difference.

Day 5 – Explore Picture Styles

Focus: Creative color and tone control

- Take a portrait, a landscape, and a close-up using three different Picture Styles (Standard, Landscape, Monochrome).

- See how the camera processes color and contrast differently without editing.

Day 6 – Low-Light Test

Focus: ISO and aperture adjustments

- Wait until evening or find a dimly lit indoor space.

- Start at ISO 100 and slowly increase it until you get a bright enough image.

- Pair a high ISO with a wide aperture (f/2.8) to keep shutter speeds reasonable.

- Learn where your personal "noise tolerance" is.

Day 7 – Try the Video Mode

Focus: Basic 4K and Full HD recording

- Record a 20–30 second clip of something simple — a pet, a meal being prepared, or traffic at sunset.

- Practice framing, panning smoothly, and keeping the subject in focus.

- Bonus: Try the touchscreen to shift focus mid-shot.

Day 8 – Capture Motion with AI Servo

Focus: Continuous autofocus for moving subjects

- Photograph a friend walking toward you or a dog running in a park.

- Use AI Servo mode and burst shooting to capture multiple frames.

- Pick the sharpest frame to understand how tracking works.

Day 9 – Experiment with Lenses

Focus: Understanding focal length impact

- Use your kit lens (18–55mm) and shoot the same subject at 18mm, 35mm, and 55mm.

- See how the background, perspective, and subject size change.

- This helps you make better lens choices for each scenario.

Day 10 – Tell a Story in 3 Shots

Focus: Creative storytelling

- Choose a theme — "Morning Routine," "Market Day," "A Walk in the Park."

- Take three photos: a wide establishing shot, a medium shot, and a close-up detail.

- Arrange them in order and see how they tell a complete visual story.

How to Get the Most from This Challenge

- Don't aim for perfection — aim for *understanding*.

- Keep all your challenge shots in a dedicated folder on your computer or memory card.

- Review them after the 10 days to see your growth.

- Repeat the challenge monthly, tweaking settings or trying new subjects.

By the end of these ten days, you'll not only know the *how* behind the Canon EOS 90D's features — you'll also instinctively know *when* to use them. That's the key to going from a hesitant beginner to a confident, capable shooter.

10-Day Photo & Video Challenge

Day 1

Find Your Perfect Grip

Steady handholding and basic composition

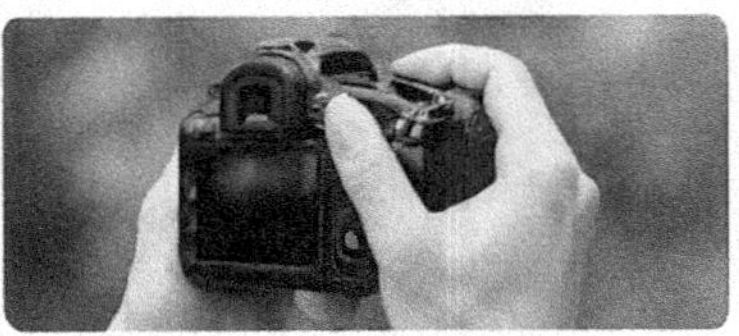

Day 2

Master Aperture Priority (Av Mode)

Depth of field control

Take 2ree shots
at different f/st.
f/8.8. f/z 6.
and 1/60 sec.

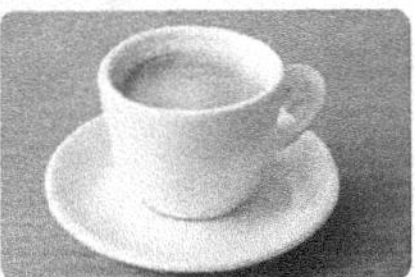

Day 3

Freeze the Action

Taking thre sics bung sujbjects

Photograph an object
with a busy backgiou-
und. Strart at
ISG 100 sec. 1/50 sec.

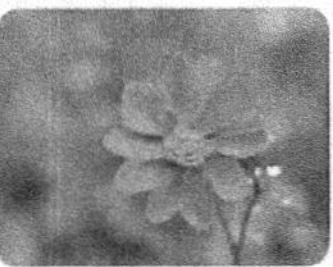

Day 4

Go Manual with Focus

Manual Focus and AF point selection

Photograph an
object with a busy
background

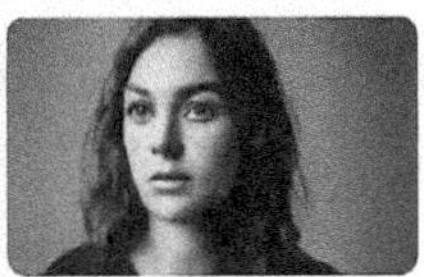

Day 5

Explore Picture Styles

Creative color and tond control

Take 3 shots using
different Picture
Styles. Start at ISO
100 in an evering
or in dimlit space

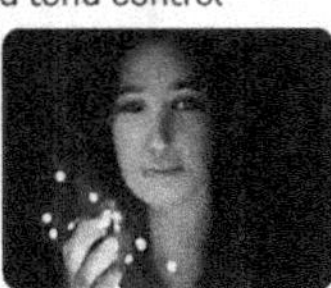

Day 8

Capture Motion with Al Servo

Continuous autofocus for moving subjects

Photograph a
person or dog
moving toward
to your

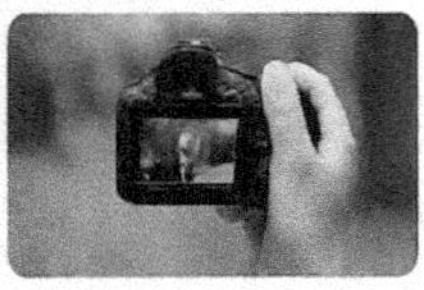

Day 7

Try the Video Mode

Basic 4K and Full HD recording

Record a 20-30 second
cilp of a simple subject

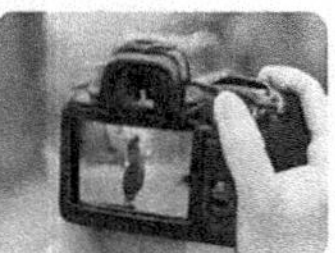

Day 9

Experiment with Lenses

Understanding focal length impact

Choose a theme
and take 3
photos. Tiree

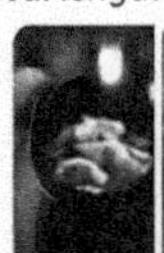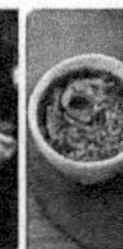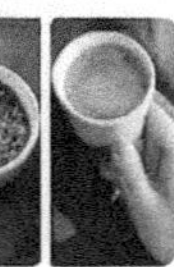

Chapter 14

Troubleshooting Common Frustrations

Even the most experienced photographers have days when their camera doesn't behave the way they expect. Whether it's a blurry shot, a mysterious memory card error, or Wi-Fi refusing to connect, these issues can steal your focus from creativity.

The good news? Most problems are simple to fix once you know why they happen and the exact steps to solve them. This chapter is your quick, confidence-boosting rescue guide for when your Canon EOS 90D tests your patience.

Blurry Photos

There's nothing worse than thinking you've nailed the shot, only to see a fuzzy mess when you zoom in. Here's why it happens — and how to stop it.

1. Camera Shake

- **Why it happens:** Shutter speed too slow to freeze your movement.
- **Fix:**
  - Use a shutter speed at least 1/your focal length (e.g., 1/100 for a 100mm lens).
  - Turn on Image Stabilization (if your lens has it).
  - Use a tripod or monopod when possible.

2. Missed Focus

- **Why it happens:** Wrong AF mode or the focus point wasn't on the subject.

- **Fix:**

    o   For still subjects → One-Shot AF.

    o   For moving subjects → AI Servo AF.

    o   Manually select a single AF point for precision.

3. Depth of Field Too Shallow

- **Why it happens:** Aperture is too wide (e.g., f/1.8), leaving very little in focus.

- **Fix:**

    o   Use f/4 to f/8 for more depth, especially in group shots.

    o   Step back slightly to increase focus range.

Grainy Images (Too Much Noise)

Noise is that speckled, sand-like texture in your photos. It's usually a side effect of high ISO or underexposure.

- **Cause #1 – High ISO:**

Shooting indoors or in low light with ISO above 3200.

- o **Fix:** Open your aperture (lower f-number) or slow your shutter speed.
- o Use a tripod to allow longer exposures without shake.

- **Cause #2 – Underexposure:**

Brightening a dark image later in editing will amplify noise.

- o **Fix:** Expose correctly in-camera by using exposure compensation.

- **Cause #3 – JPEG Compression:**

Shooting only in JPEG can introduce compression artifacts.

- o **Fix:** Shoot in RAW for higher quality and cleaner edits.

Memory Card Errors

Memory card failures can lead to lost shots or total inability to save images.

- **Problem:** *"Card Cannot Be Accessed" or "Card Error"*

  o **Fix:**

    - Turn off the camera and remove/reinsert the card.

    - Use only high-speed, Class 10 or UHS-I/UHS-II SD cards from reputable brands.

    - If the error persists, format the card in-camera (Menu $\rightarrow$ Format Card). Warning: This erases all data.

- **Problem:** *"Card Full" in the Middle of Shooting*

  o **Fix:**

    - Keep a spare card in your bag.

    - Transfer and back up files regularly.

    - Reduce file size settings only as a last resort.

Pro Tip: Always format cards in your camera before use, not on your computer.

Wi-Fi Connection Problems

The Canon EOS 90D's Wi-Fi feature makes transferring images and remote shooting easy — when it works.

- **Common Cause #1 – Wrong Network Settings**
  - **Fix:**
    - Delete the existing connection in your camera's Wi-Fi menu.
    - Reconnect by following the on-screen guide.
- **Common Cause #2 – App Issues**
  - **Fix:**
    - Ensure the Canon Camera Connect app is updated.
    - Restart your phone and camera before reconnecting.
- **Common Cause #3 – Interference**
  - **Fix:**

- Avoid crowded Wi-Fi environments (cafes, events).

- If possible, connect using Bluetooth first, then switch to Wi-Fi.

Video Playback Issues

You've recorded a great video, but it won't play smoothly — or at all.

- **Problem:** Video stutters or skips during playback.
  - **Cause:** Your computer or device may not handle high-bitrate 4K smoothly.
  - **Fix:** Lower the resolution to Full HD for easier playback or upgrade your playback device.
- **Problem:** "File Cannot Be Played" on Camera
  - **Cause:** Recording was interrupted (e.g., dead battery or full card).

- o **Fix:** Try playing the file on a computer with video repair software.

  Note: Sometimes corrupted clips can't be saved.

- **Problem:** No Sound in Video Playback

  - o **Cause:** External mic not fully inserted or muted.

  - o **Fix:** Double-check audio settings before shooting and monitor with headphones.

Final Tip – Stay Ahead of Problems

Most frustrations with the Canon EOS 90D are preventable with:

- Regular gear maintenance.

- Backups before important shoots.

- Testing settings before events.

- Carrying spares: batteries, cards, cables.

With this troubleshooting toolkit, you can fix issues on the spot and get back to doing what matters most — capturing the shot.

TROUBLESHOOTING COMMON FRUSTRATIONS

BLURRY PHOTOS

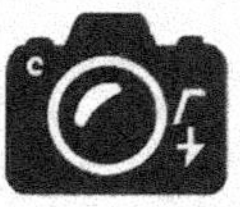

– A: Use afaster shutter speed
- Image stabilizational

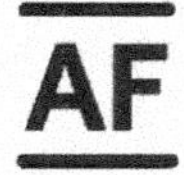

– A: Missed depth of field
- Use a narrover aperture

– Shallow depth of field

GRAINY IMOSES

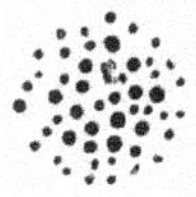

Excessive noise
- Use lower ISO value
- Wider aperture

Adjust exposure
- Adjust exposure s
- Check

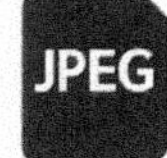

JPEG compression
- Shoot in RAW

MEMORY CARD ERRORS

Card Cannot Be Accessed

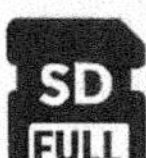

- Reinsert or format
- Card

– Card Full
- Use addition card

WI-FI CONNECTION PROBLEMS

Lower resolution
- Reconfigure Wi-Fi function

App issues
- Update camera connect app

VIDEO PLAYBACK ISSUES

Stuttering
- Lower resolution for smoother playback

File cannot be played
- Attempt repair

VIDEO PLAYBACK ISSUES

Stuttering
- Lower resolution for smooth

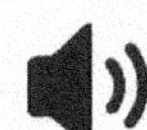

No sound
- Check microp

Appendices

Quick Reference Settings – Large Print Edition

Sometimes you don't have the time—or the light—to scroll through your entire menu or flip through pages to figure out what settings you need. This quick reference section is designed to be your "fast lane" to great results. Think of it as your pocket-sized memory aid in words, not tables.

For Bright Outdoor Days (Travel, Landscapes, Street Photography)

- **Mode:** Aperture Priority (Av)
- **Aperture:** f/8 for sharpness front to back
- **ISO:** 100 (lowest for best quality)
- **Autofocus:** One-Shot AF, single point for stationary subjects
- **White Balance:** Daylight

For Low-Light Indoors (Family Gatherings, Indoor Events)

- **Mode:** Aperture Priority (Av)

- **Aperture:** f/2.8–f/4 for more light in

- **ISO:** 1600–3200 (keeps shutter speed fast enough to avoid

  blur)

- **Autofocus:** One-Shot AF with Eye Detection

- **White Balance:** Auto or Tungsten for warm lights

For Fast-Moving Subjects (Kids, Pets, Sports)

- **Mode:** Shutter Priority (Tv)

- **Shutter Speed:** 1/1000s or faster

- **ISO:** Auto (with a limit of 3200)

- **Autofocus:** AI Servo AF with continuous tracking

- **Drive Mode:** High-Speed Continuous Shooting

For Video Recording

- **Resolution:** 4K at 24 or 30fps for cinematic look

- **Shutter Speed:** Double your frame rate (e.g., 1/60s for 30fps)

- **ISO:** Auto with upper limit 1600 for cleaner footage

- **Autofocus:** Movie Servo AF with Face + Tracking

Photography Glossary

Aperture – The adjustable opening in your lens that lets in light. Think of it like your eye's pupil: big opening for more light, small opening for less.

Shutter Speed – How long your camera's "eye" stays open. Fast speeds freeze action, slow speeds blur motion.

ISO – How sensitive your camera is to light. Lower ISO = cleaner image, higher ISO = more visible grain.

Bokeh – The soft, blurry background you get when your subject is in focus but the background melts away.

White Balance – A setting that makes colors look natural under different lighting (sunlight, indoor bulbs, etc.).

RAW File – A high-quality image file that keeps all the details for editing, unlike JPEG which compresses data.

Autofocus Points – Small zones your camera uses to decide where to focus.

Burst Mode – Taking multiple shots in rapid succession by holding down the shutter button.

Metering – How the camera measures light to decide exposure.

Depth of Field – How much of your photo is sharp from front to back.

Resource List – Gear & Tools to Help You Grow

Recommended Lenses

- **Canon EF-S 18–135mm IS USM** – Great all-rounder for travel, portraits, and landscapes.
- **Canon EF 50mm f/1.8 STM** – Affordable, sharp, and perfect for portraits and low light.

- **Canon EF-S 10–18mm IS STM** – Great for wide landscapes, interiors, and vlogging.

Audio Gear for Video

- **Rode VideoMicro** – Compact, plug-and-play microphone for cleaner sound.
- **Rode Wireless GO II** – For wireless audio when filming interviews or moving subjects.

Tripods & Stabilization

- **Manfrotto Compact Action Tripod** – Lightweight and beginner-friendly.
- **Joby GorillaPod 3K** – Flexible legs for uneven surfaces and vlogging setups.

Cleaning Tools

- **LensPen** – Pocket-sized tool for lens smudges.

- **Rocket Air Blower** – Safe dust removal from the sensor and lens.

Free Editing Software

- **Canon Digital Photo Professional (DPP)** – Comes with your camera for editing RAW files.

- **GIMP** – Free Photoshop alternative for advanced editing.

- **DaVinci Resolve** – Free video editing software with professional features.

APPENDICES

Quick Reference Settings – Large Print

For Bright Outdoor Days (Travel, Landscapes, Street Photography)

- Aperrture Priority (Av)
- f/8 for sharpness front t to back
- ISO 100 (for oest quality)
- One-Shot AF single point for stationary subjects for avoid blur
- One-Shot AF with EyeDetection Auto or Tungsten

For Fast-Moving Subjects (Kids, Pets, Sports)

- Shutter Priority (Tv)
- 1/1000s or faster
- ISO ( )with a limit of (x der 3200)
- AI Servo AF with continuous tracking
- Drive Mode: Hgh-Spleoous Shooting

For Video Recording

- 4K Resolution– 24 or 30fps for cinematic look
- Shutter Speed: domle your frame rate (e g, 1/60s for 30fps)
- ISO with upper limit 160500
  Movie Servo AF
  with Face+Tracking

For Video Recording

- 4K Resolution 24 or 30fps for cinematic look
- ISO (with a limit of 3/00) for cleaner footage
- Movie Servo AF

Photography Glossary – In Plain English

- **Resolution**: A bujastade opening in the lens that lets in light
- **Shutter Speed**: Double your frame rate (e.g.. 1/60s for 30, fast speeds freeze action, slow spee ds blur motion
- **ISO**: with uppernon limit 1600 for cleaner footage
- **Autofocus**: AI with Fac + Tracking Autofocus

Resource List – Gear & Tools to Help You Grow

- **Recommended Lenses**
  Canon EF-5 18–155mm IS USM
  Great all-rounder for travel, port-traits and landscapes
- **Canon EF 50mm I 1 8 STM**
  Affordable. sharp perfecfect for portraits and low light
- **Canon EF-5 10–18mm FS STM**
  For wide landscapes, interiors, and vlogging
- **Cleaning Tools**
  LensPen, apocketsized toöi for lons smudges
- **Rocket Air Blower**, safe dust removal from the sensor / lens
- **Free Edtting Software**
  Canon Digital Photo Preössional (DPP) included with co Gasson for editing RAW files
- **DaVinci Resolve** Free video editing software with professional

Acknowledgments

Creating this guide has been a journey made possible by more than just technical know-how—it's been powered by community, curiosity, and countless moments behind the lens.

First, to the everyday photographers—beginners, seniors, travelers, vloggers, and creators—who inspired this book: thank you. Your questions, frustrations, and breakthroughs shaped every chapter and reminded me why clarity matters.

To the online communities, forum contributors, and real-world Canon EOS 90D users who openly shared their challenges and insights: your stories breathed realism into this work.

A special thanks to my editorial team, design collaborators, and research assistants for helping bring structure, precision, and visual support to every page.

Finally, to the readers picking up this book—whether you're just unboxing your Canon 90D or finally ready to leave auto mode behind—thank you for trusting this guide as part of your journey. May it help you create images that not only look beautiful, but feel meaningful.

Keep shooting. Keep learning. The world is waiting through your lens.

About The Author

Randy Osborn is a trusted name in the world of camera education, known for transforming complex gear manuals into simple, step-by-step guides that anyone can understand. With over a decade of experience working hands-on with leading camera systems—from Sony and Canon to Nikon, Leica, and more—Randy has helped thousands of photographers, content creators, and everyday users get the most out of their cameras without the overwhelm.

Driven by a passion for accessible learning, Randy creates user-friendly books that strip away the jargon and focus on real-world usage. Whether you're shooting your first vlog, learning manual mode for the first time, or simply trying to take better family photos, Randy's guides are designed to make every setting click.

Each book combines clear instruction, practical tips, and

relatable language, making it easy for beginners and seasoned hobbyists alike to master their gear and capture life with confidence.

When he's not writing, Randy enjoys field testing new camera releases, hosting beginner-friendly workshops, and exploring hidden photography gems across the globe.

Join the journey to sharper skills and smarter shooting—one page at a time.